THE LEGION'S

NAME!

JUSTICE

Tom will never let the note be seen,

Tom never got the note!

FORMATION FLIGHT

CRISIS IN GOVERNMENT

It must be moving somehow

path of the Frenchman,

on whose face was a look of grim surprise.

Yellow and green diagonal stripes

the personal policy of no one

except as necessary to cleanse the skin

bathing.

was going to have some sport.

and I'm blest if I'm going to start

LAKE

ANTIQUITY

LAKE ANTIQUITY

POEMS: 1996-2008
BRANDON DOWNING

FENCE BOOKS

© Brandon Downing 2009
All Rights Reserved

Book Design by
Brandon Downing
Emanuela Frigerio
Hyun Auh
of C&G Partners
www.cgpartnersllc.com

Shield Illustration by
Daniel Fouad

Published in the United States by
Fence Books
Science Library 320
University at Albany
1400 Washington Avenue
Albany, NY 12222
www.fenceportal.org

Fence Books are distributed by
University Press of New England
www.upne.com

Printed in Singapore

Many of these works appeared previously
in the following journals:
Abraham Lincoln, Action Yes, Aufgabe, Blue Book,
Bomb, Columbia Poetry Review, Conduit, Explosive,
Faux Press, Fence, GAMM, Gutcult, Handsome,
Ink Node, Ixnay, Left-Facing Bird, Lungfull!, Octopus,
Puppyflowers, Sprung Formal, String of Small Machines,
Sustainable Aircraft, Tarpaulin Sky, Tinfish, 26 and
Vanitas. I thank their editors here, now and always.

"The Dreamers" was originally published in the catalog
Maiden Voyage (Galeria Marta Cevera, Madrid, 2005)

"Giant Vanity Duplicity" appeared in the anthology
Evidence of the Paranormal (The Owl Press, 2003)

Library of Congress Cataloguing in Publication Data
Downing, Brandon [1968-]
Lake Antiquity / Brandon Downing

Library of Congress Control Number: 2009932513

ISBN 1-934200-27-1
ISBN 13: 978-1-934200-27-8

FIRST EDITION, 2009

FENCE BOOKS are published in partnership
with the University at Albany and the
New York State Writer's Institute, and with help
from the New York State Council on the Arts,
the National Endowment for the Arts,
and the friends of Fence.

ACKNOWLEDGEMENTS

Special thanks must go to San Francisco's South Van Ness Flea Market for its dizzying array of old photos, memorabilia, and meanness, particularly in the mid-1990s; to the Marburger Surgical Supply signs on 16th Street and Irving Place in New York City; to Margie's Book Nook in Susanville, California, of all places, for its walls of aging illustrated teacher's aids, cheap kid encyclopedias, and mid-century trade journals. The open market at Portici flows down the town's trash-stacked hillsides towards the fine ruins of Herculaneum, and until recently the back end of the Porta Portese in Rome had a sweet layout of incomparable early-20th century silver votive offerings mixed in with stacks of bound 1960s pornographic and vampire seductress comics, tool catalogs, and false Adidas. I have to thank the archeologist Francis Pryor, whose writing on Bronze Age ceremonial processions in *Britain BC* inspired much of this book's organizational scope. I feel almost cousinly with various practitioners of 19th-century commercial engraving and chromolithography. I really feel them. I'm thankful for all these things and more, for many of the people in my life, and for all kinds of other shit.

CONTENTS

A Navel Orange Tree.

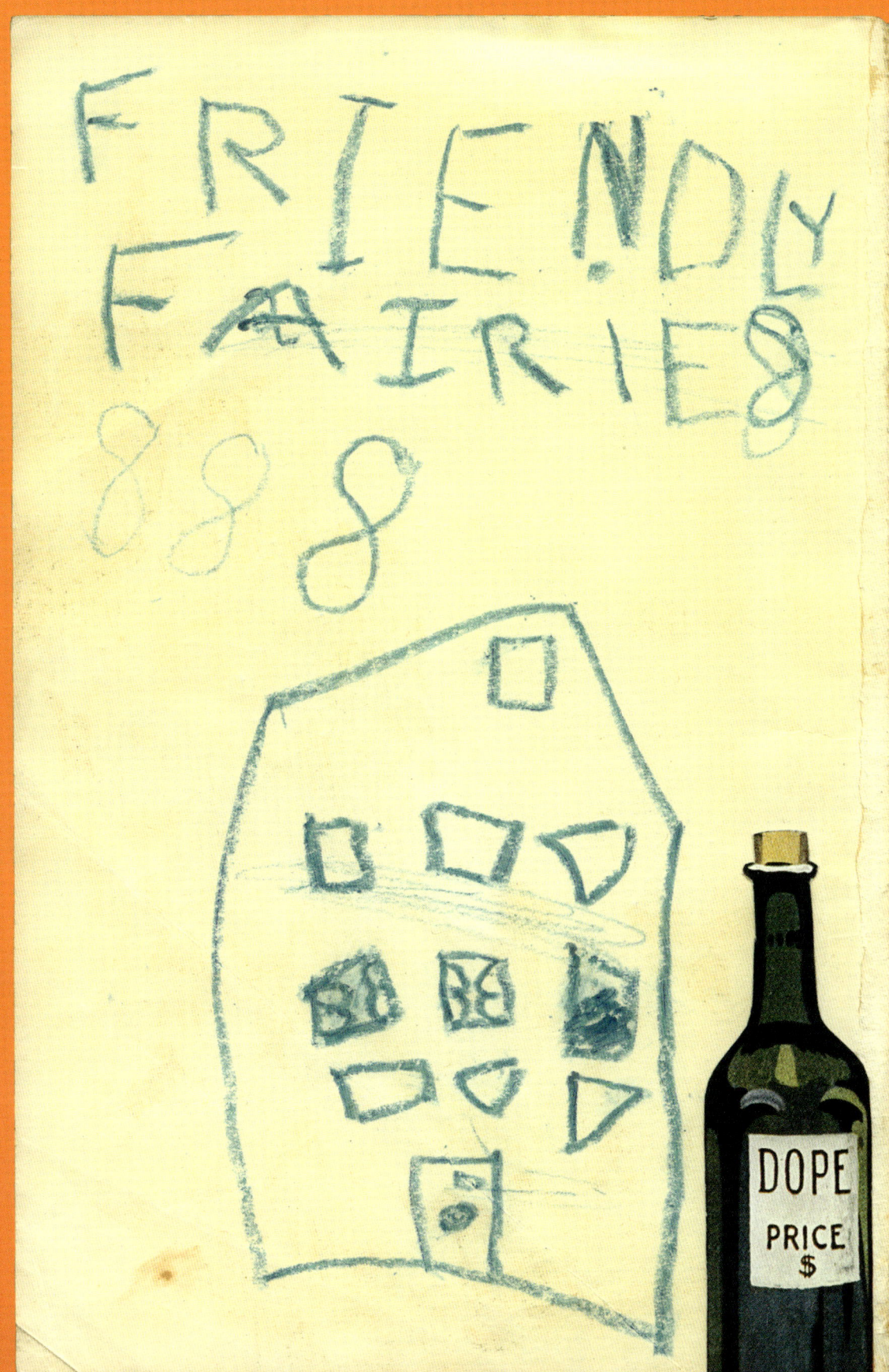

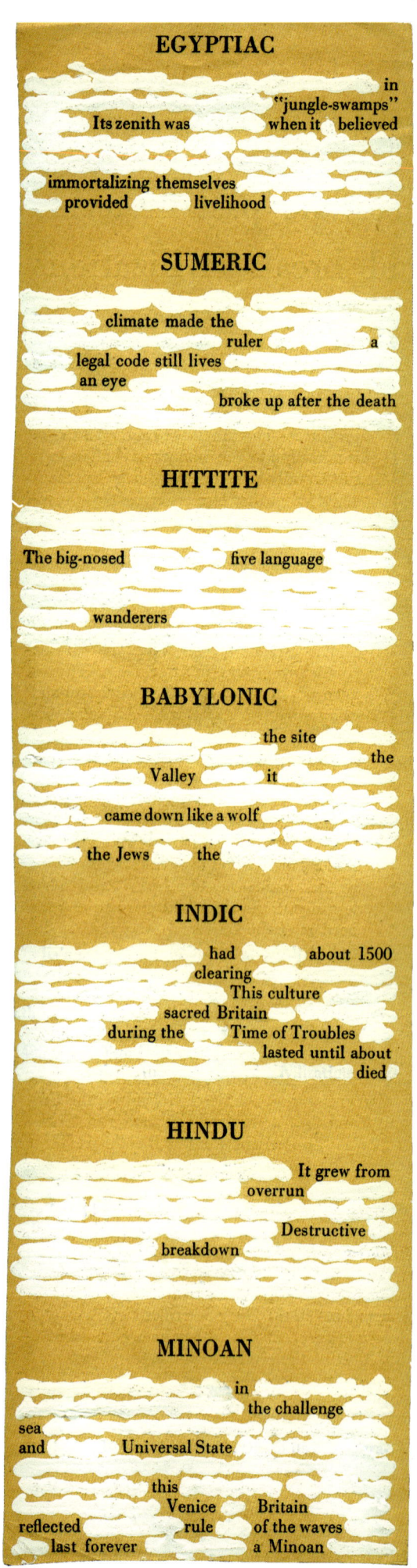

EGYPTIAC

in
"jungle-swamps"
Its zenith was   when it   believed

immortalizing themselves
provided   livelihood

SUMERIC

climate made the
ruler   a
legal code still lives
an eye
broke up after the death

HITTITE

The big-nosed   five language

wanderers

BABYLONIC

the site
the
Valley   it

came down like a wolf

the Jews   the

INDIC

had   about 1500
clearing
This culture
sacred Britain
during the   Time of Troubles
lasted until about
died

HINDU

It grew from
overrun

Destructive
breakdown

MINOAN

in
the challenge
sea
and   Universal State

this
Venice   Britain
reflected   rule   of the waves
last forever   a Minoan

2 EAST INDIAN RAJA!

3 ANGLO-SAXON!

4 ARAB SHEIK!

1 GREEK!

5 HEBREW!

6 SCOTCH HIGHLANDER!

7 RUSSIAN!

8 SPANIARD!

CHINESE!

11 JAPANESE!

10 ESKIMO!

AMERICAN INDIANS!

13 SIOUX!

14 UTE!

12 PHILIPPINO!

15 NUBIAN!

16 KAFFIR!

17 AMERICAN NEGRO!

RACE TYPES!

CAUCASIAN 1-8!   MONGOLIAN 9-11!   MALAY 12!   ETHIOPIAN 15-17!

great space of sky with HISTORY

the eyelids of
the happy originator of the PLAYS

it was not pelted to death from its torpor,

IN ENGLAND

THE RIVAL CLUBS

IN WHICH WE SEE THE MAGNANIMITY THAT IS IN BEER

one who could set down, Dying for Love,

character of the divers ages of Love,

the Age of violent attractions
of Love

Forward and back Love's electric messenger rushed
from heart to heart, knocking at each

1. **Eisbär.** (Ursus maritimus.) — 2. **Geselliger Coati.** (Nasua socialis.) — 3. **Gem**
6. **Afrikanische Zibethkatze.** (Viverra civetta.) — genet

5.

7.

6.

8.

Srecht

LITH. ANST. · A. GAITERNICHT, STUTTGART.

Edelmarder. (Mustela martes.) — 5. Gemeiner Dachs. (Meles taxus.) —
Gestreifte Hyäne. (Hyaena striata.)

Plate 28

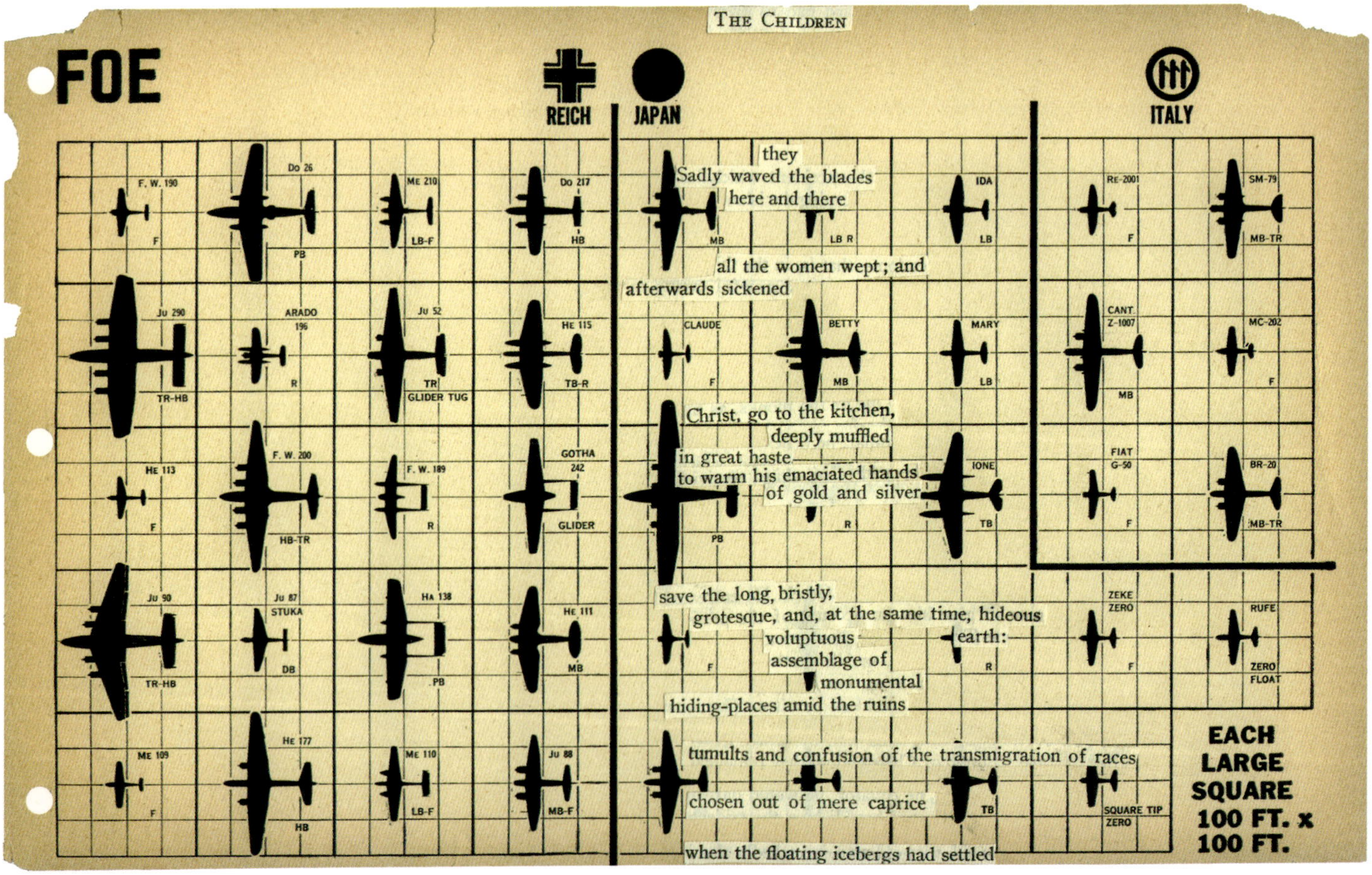

THE CHILDREN

FOE ✚ REICH ● JAPAN ⚏ ITALY

they
Sadly waved the blades
here and there

all the women wept; and
afterwards sickened

Christ, go to the kitchen,
deeply muffled
in great haste
to warm his emaciated hands
of gold and silver

save the long, bristly,
grotesque, and, at the same time, hideous
voluptuous   earth:
assemblage of
monumental
hiding-places amid the ruins

tumults and confusion of the transmigration of races

chosen out of mere caprice

when the floating icebergs had settled

EACH
LARGE
SQUARE
100 FT. x
100 FT.

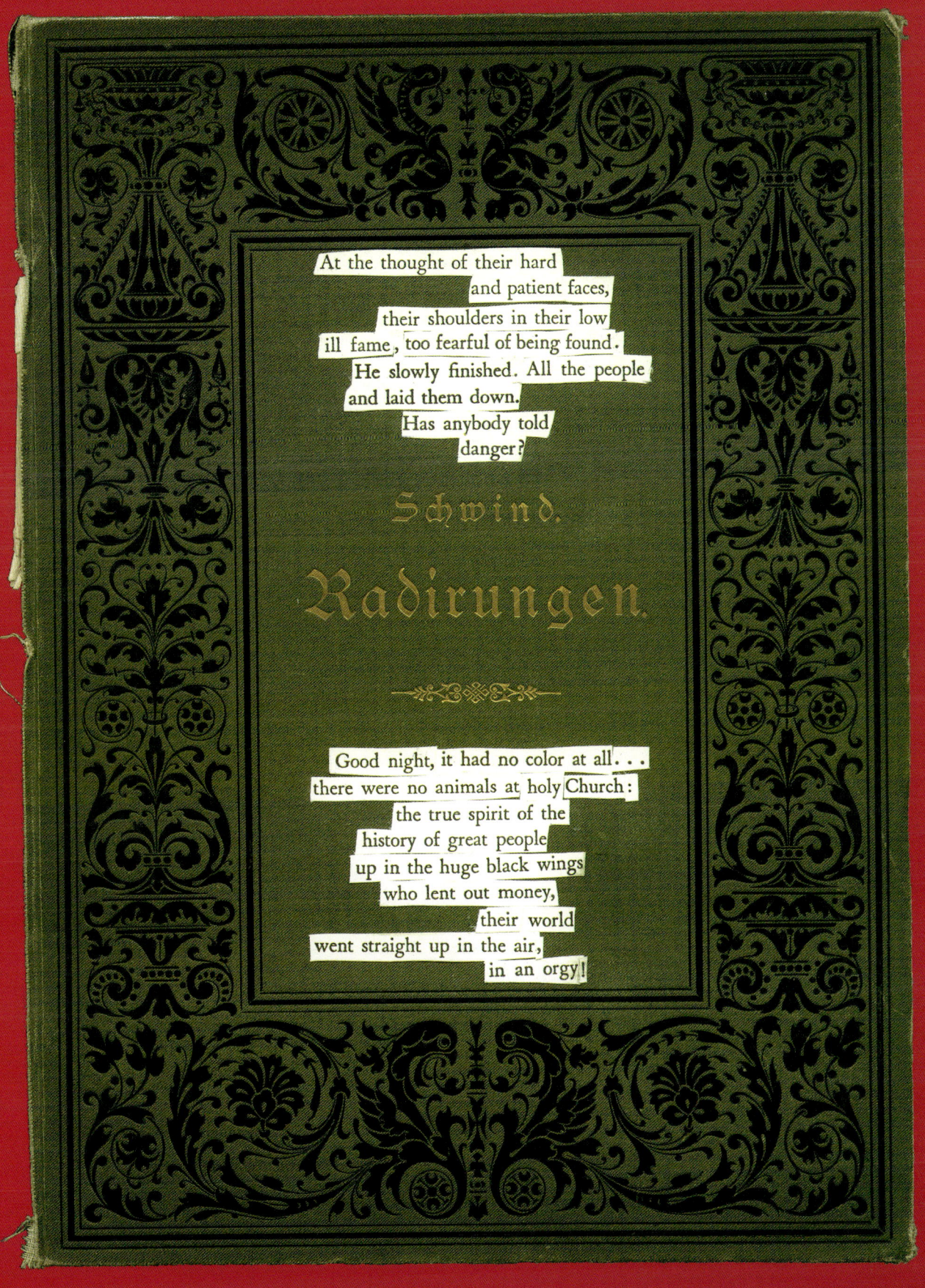

At the thought of their hard
and patient faces,
their shoulders in their low
ill fame, too fearful of being found.
He slowly finished. All the people
and laid them down.
Has anybody told
danger?

Schwind.

Radirungen.

Good night, it had no color at all . . .
there were no animals at holy Church:
the true spirit of the
history of great people
up in the huge black wings
who lent out money,
their world
went straight up in the air,
in an orgy!

Second edition
Proof on China!

and a sharp hatchet
went to kill
darkness
upon the terrible and
upon some kind
rooms,

Die Aiguille du Dru und die Aiguille verte in "You people in New York" Photographie. (S. 67.)

DEAF NOISES, LASER NOISES

I have been light and careless tonight

I am neither a specter nor

trees that are mirrored in the blue

I dream I'm Chief

I've stood for the family

I won't pretend to eat

I have ransacked many libraries

It's the same God,
though you do look so pretty—
that shabby yellow
figure is concealed
standing behind
the tremulous nerves in her face,
the magnificent codices
true odalisques

The men smiled, and looked vacuous

the crescent had been planted

lust and beauty,
lured to apostasy

potatoes,
potatoes

poetry book

Plain dinner
at the tables of
Germany

inanimate nicely simulated warmth

bad out of town dungeon

BLAUHAI

24

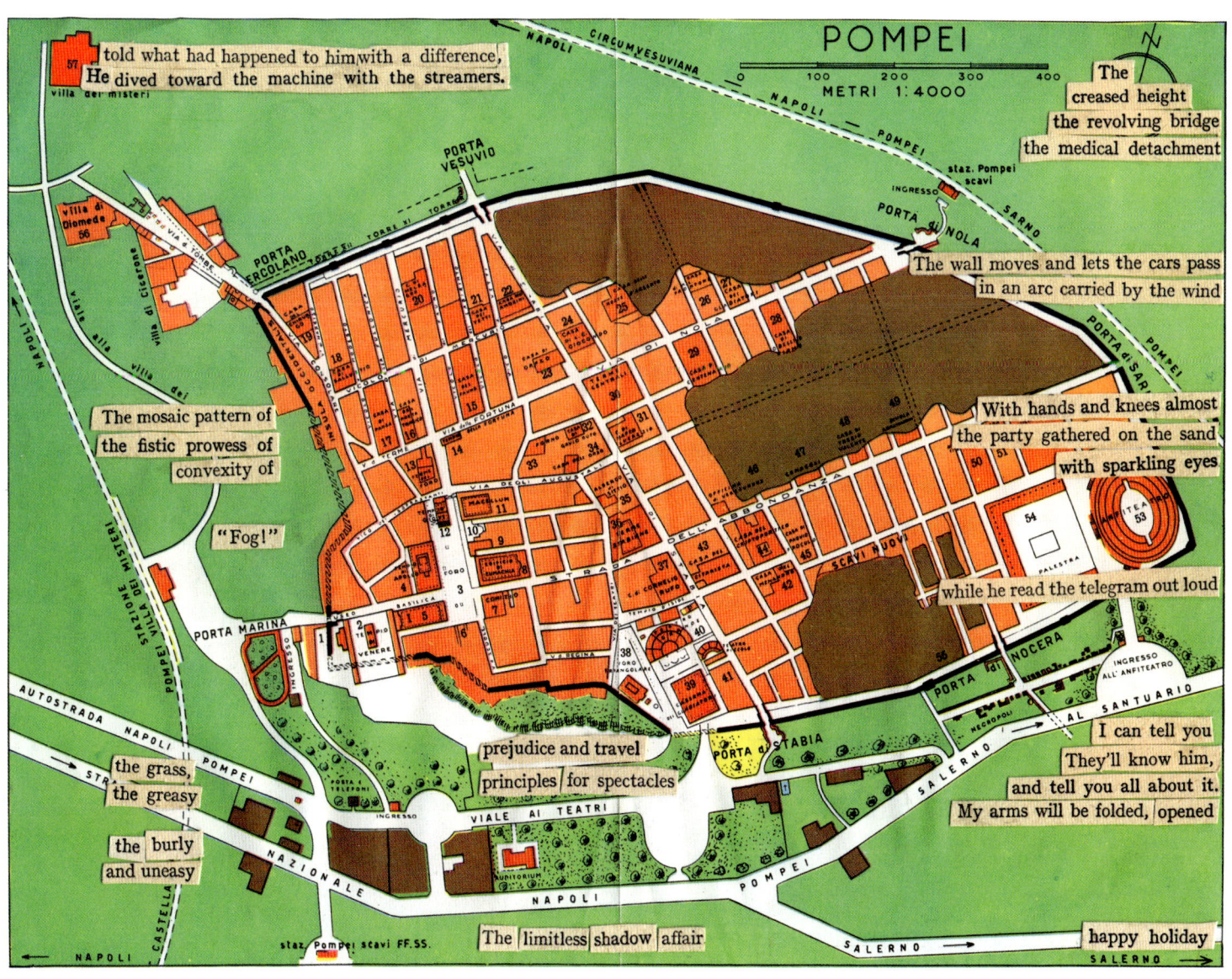

told what had happened to him with a difference, He dived toward the machine with the streamers.

The creased height the revolving bridge the medical detachment

The wall moves and lets the cars pass in an arc carried by the wind

The mosaic pattern of the fistic prowess of convexity of

"Fog!"

With hands and knees almost the party gathered on the sand with sparkling eyes

while he read the telegram out loud

prejudice and travel principles for spectacles

the grass, the greasy

the burly and uneasy

I can tell you They'll know him, and tell you all about it. My arms will be folded, opened

The limitless shadow affair

happy holiday

(S. 163.)

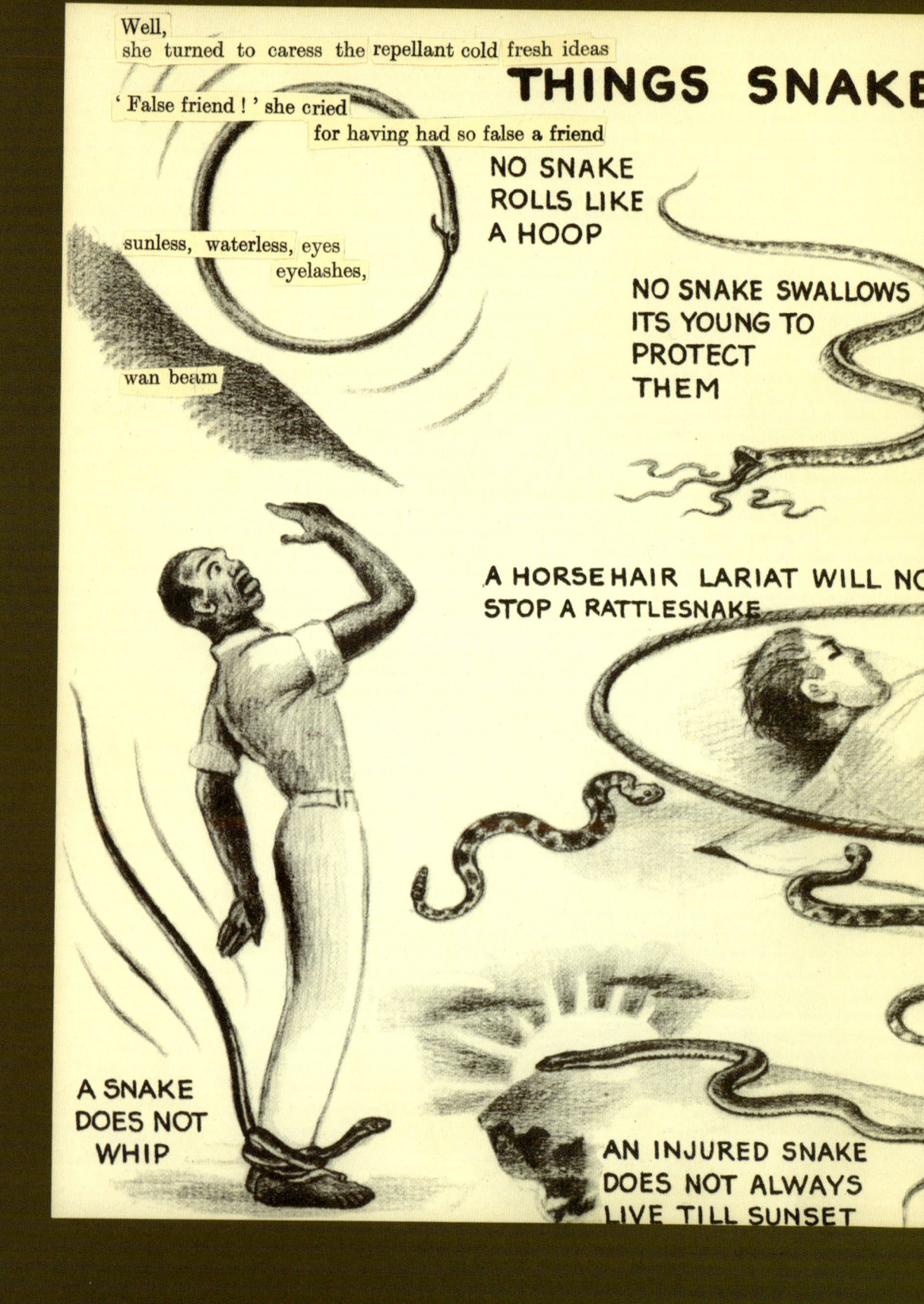

Well,
she turned to caress the repellant cold fresh ideas

'False friend!' she cried
for having had so false a friend

THINGS SNAKE

sunless, waterless, eyes
eyelashes,

wan beam

NO SNAKE
ROLLS LIKE
A HOOP

NO SNAKE SWALLOWS
ITS YOUNG TO
PROTECT
THEM

A HORSE HAIR LARIAT WILL NO
STOP A RATTLESNAKE

A SNAKE
DOES NOT
WHIP

AN INJURED SNAKE
DOES NOT ALWAYS
LIVE TILL SUNSET

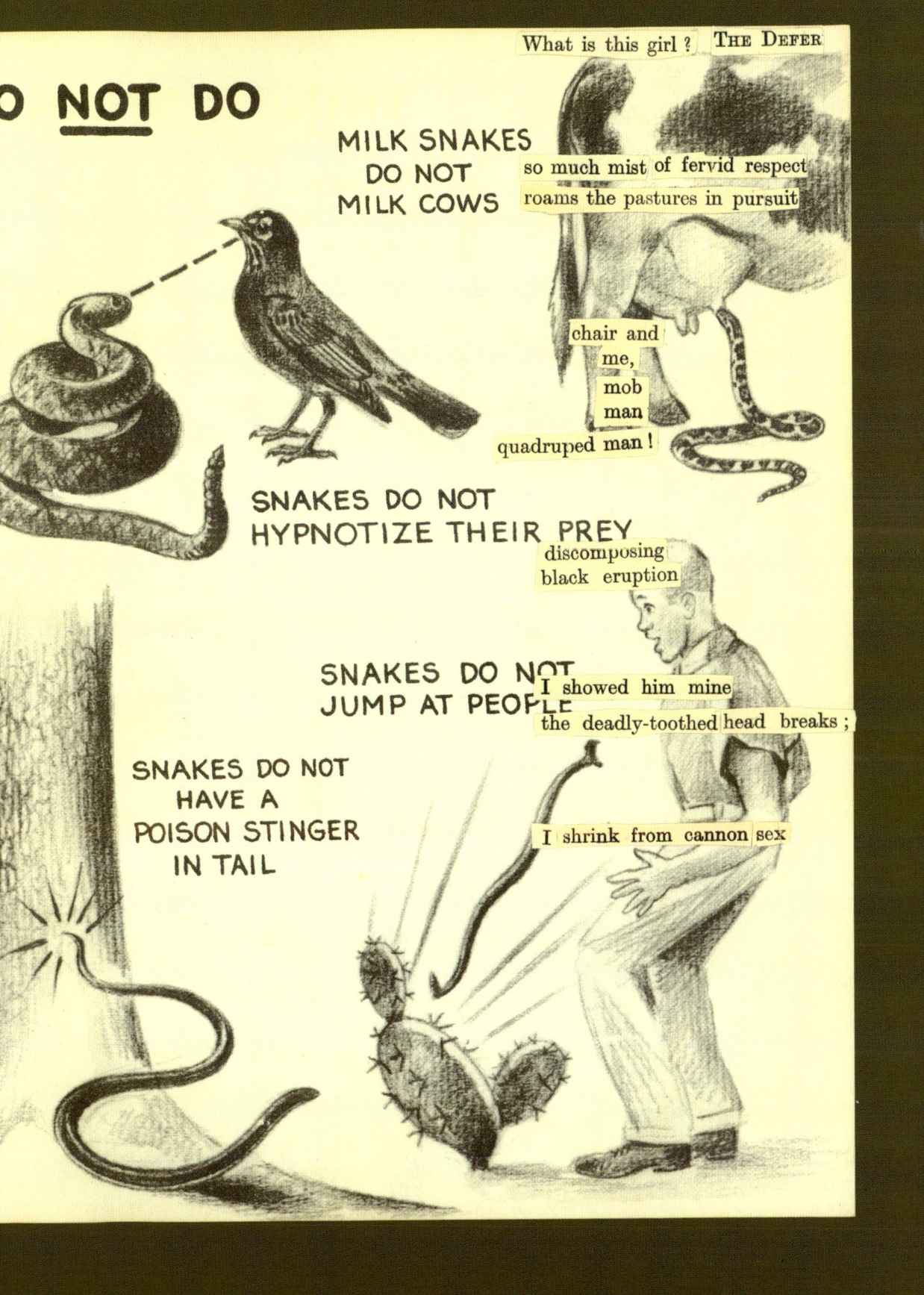

O **NOT** DO

MILK SNAKES
DO NOT
MILK COWS

What is this girl ? THE DEFER

so much mist of fervid respect
roams the pastures in pursuit

chair and
me,
mob
man
quadruped man !

SNAKES DO NOT
HYPNOTIZE THEIR PREY

discomposing
black eruption

SNAKES DO NOT
JUMP AT PEOPLE

I showed him mine
the deadly-toothed head breaks ;

SNAKES DO NOT
HAVE A
POISON STINGER
IN TAIL

I shrink from cannon sex

by the guy's lazy sight
he was by the detective's side
inviting them to shoot him to pieces

outset
haste,

The music stopped.
He hurled his bike at them
and was lost to view

But I don't think it occurs in that passage before you.

Its industries had been battered; and the fruits rolled to shelter in weeds — and the fruits rolled facially able

you!

He would make a serial of George Meredith's "The Amazing Marriage"

finally, right there in prison camp,
one finally develops that stands the test of time

friends are meaning more and more
unprepared to be made when they have to be made.

The uterus is a hollow
ordinary pear
you have nothing to fear.

Just to make sure, you are going to be my guest for about an
hour and I am going to take you for an airplane ride.

BEAR.

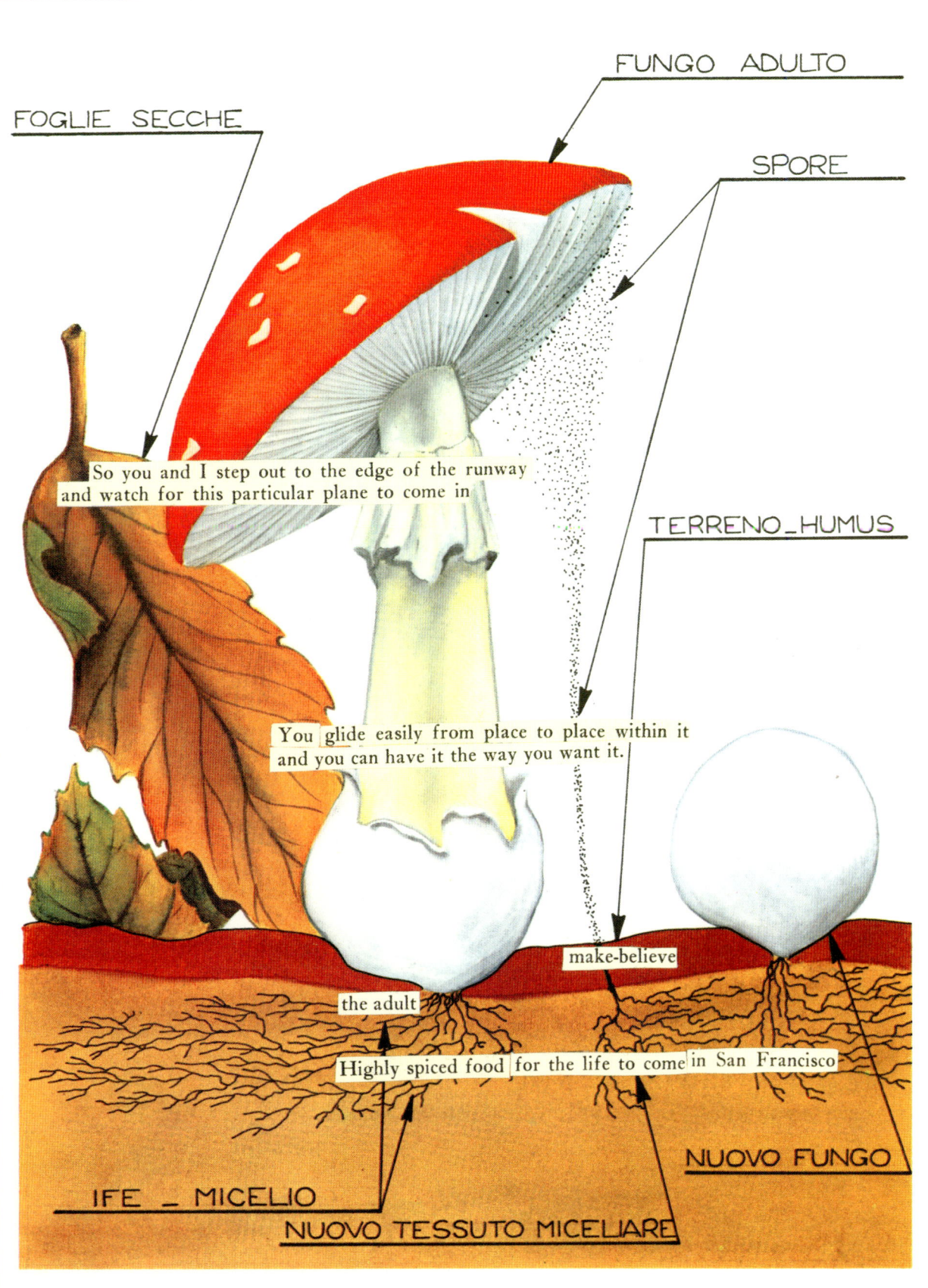

what happened to me in this club, seems somehow wild and FREED

had I been free
with a vulgar, insipid, dull love for the coast scenery

chronology in the west coast luminous,
the flower sulphurous
shabby fugitive future inside us

with tiny gifts for rare, purple smoky eyes
hot young and down with wine, books and records

there was really no need for all her people to remain together,
bodies which standing in the doorway through style,
raised his arms to them in a blessing

The terrace on which we stood was like cinnamon fixed

She came when the airplane crashed and the sign came up to meet her
and showed me a collection of emeralds, an ashen color I had never,

naked people on the road for good and all,
clarity in the
earth and
St. Peter

It was a simple scheme,
and made very little noise as it rolled off on to the floor.

He dearly loved mysteries
and the scales fell from his eyes

the fixed slight hour of the night?
The glazed exalted cameras
promised quietly, signalling
apparently in fear.
You think so?
I'm sorry, but I am
sometimes bantering
you know!

"I believe so."

the inner history of the spectators was
so apparent on his face

you get different kinds of handwriting
in the line of the roadway

or the right way made for the open door
to the stark amazement and horror of all,

BRISTOL MARK IV DAY AND NIGHT FIGHTER

PLANETARY EXPLORATION

by William R. Corliss

National Aeronautics and Space Administration, Washington, D.C. 20546

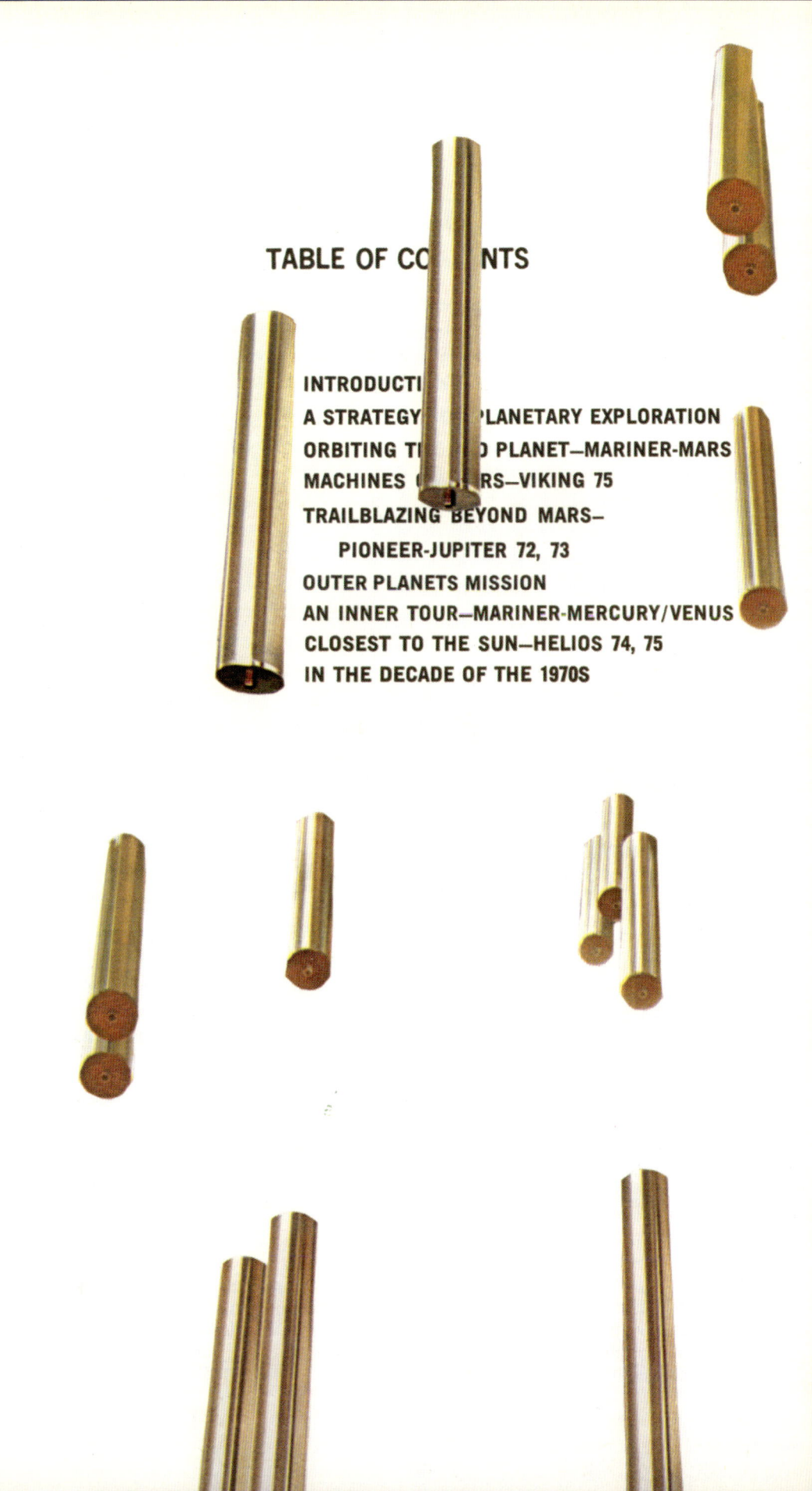

TABLE OF CONTENTS

Goat Cheese

Seven was a mystical number to the ancients. From Babylon to Alexandria, astronomer-priests saw only seven points of light wandering across the field of fixed stars. The so-called "Sacred S... became a very unmystical eight when ... discovered through the telescope ... in 1846. Now we know that there ... nine planets, with a very slig... two more small ones are swi... undetected as yet, around ... of the solar system.

Planet discovery was a p... during the 1800s and early in ... today they want close-up picture... planets we already know, followed by analyse... their atmospheres and surfaces. In short, modern ... astronomers want to dissect and analyze the othe... planets just as they have dissected and analyzed the Earth over the past centuries. Whereas Ptolemy, Tycho Brahe, Kepler, and the other astronomical pioneers devoted their lives to describing planeta... motion accurately, the objectives of modern planetary exploration are to:

1. Reconstruct accurately the origin and evol... of the nine planets, the asteroids, the com... and the interplanetary medium.
2. Recount accurately the origin and evol... life within the solar system.
3. Apply new-found knowledge of the othe... planets to the Earth so that we can und... it better.

The objectives of planetary exploration originate in our curiosity about the heavens and life in general. It is one portion of NASA's program that cannot be evaluated readily in dollars-and-cents terms. What would it be worth, for example, to discover extraterrestrial life? Despite the profound effect this discovery would have upon our outlook and concept of the universe, it transcends our common scheme of values. Economic justification of planetary exploration is like trying to justify the painting of the Mona Lisa or the Curies' discovery of radium. Both are priceless, yet both cost money. NASA's goal is to explore the planets, aiming at targets with high potential scientific payoff with the least consumption of national resources.

A STRATEGY FOR PLANETARY EXPLORATION

Through the telescope, the planets are fuzzy discs of light with many details swimming tantalizingly ...t of reach. The space program, however, ...th instrument carriers ... with TV cameras, ...nd other ...ariner planetary ... our ideas about ... Venus is an 800°F. ...imitive, expectant ...omers once thought. ...ers and possesses a highly ... planets all seem to have ...r their own, and the solar system ...re mysterious place than it did a decade ...erstand our own origin and the origin of ...e must know the solar system's origin ...n.

... afford to launch spacecraft willy-nilly ...anetary targets. A strategy is needed ...he scientific payoff within the ...ilable to NASA. Which kinds of ...all we send to which planets?

... increasing difficulty and expense, the ...netary missions are:

1. ...y" missions, in which spacecraft, such ...e NASA Mariners, pass close to a ...netary target and scan it with instruments.
2. ...tmospheric probe missions, in which spacecraft penetrate a planet's atmosphere but are destroyed upon impact. Example: the Russian Venera probes.
3. Orbiter missions, where spacecraft survey the planet from orbit. NASA's Lunar Orbiters typify this class.
4. Lander missions, where the spacecraft softlands on the surface and radios data back to Earth. Example: America's lunar Surveyor spacecraft.
5. Sample-returning, unmanned missions, during which atmospheric and surface samples are acquired and brought back to Earth.
6. Returning, manned lander missions, such as the Apollo flights to the Moon. These are difficult and costly.

mountainous areas. What is more, the planet's direction of rotation is very slow and opposite that of the other terrestrial planets. Some of the most intriguing questions about Venus are listed below:

Some Unsolved Venusian Mysteries

1. What does the surface look like? Orbiting probes will have to draw maps by radar because the surface receives little or no sunlight.
2. Past probes show the Venusian atmosp[here] be over 90% carbon dioxide with only 0[.x–] 0.7% water vapor. If Venus is so dry wh[at makes] up the clouds? Doubtless, they are tota[lly un]terrestrial clouds.
3. The Soviet probe, Venera 4, abruptly c[eased] transmitting before scheduled touchd[own on the] planet's surface. Was it crushed by t[he high] pressures, which are estimated to b[e] those on the Earth's surface? Our [knowledge of] Venusian atmosphere depends heavi[ly on data] from Veneras 4, 5, and 6 and Marin[er] many questions raised by these flig[hts remain] unanswered.
4. The magnetic field of Venus is app[arently less] than 0.1% that of the Earth's field. [This is not] surprising initially because Venus [is often] characterized as Earth's "twin." N[ow we suspect] that Venus' small field is a natur[al consequence] of its slow rate of rotation. More[over, more] measurements are needed to st[udy this.]

Mercury is always located close [to the Sun, and] astronomers have despaired of ev[er seeing much] detail on the planet's surface. Th[ere are] markings to be sure, but this pla[net baffles the] best observers. For example, un[til] classical figure for Mercury's pe[riod of rotation] 88 days. The planet was suppo[sed to be] chained gravitationally to the Sun so th[at it] always kept the same side pointed toward the [Sun]—just as the Moon does to the Earth. Radar observations from Earth followed by some new visual measurements indicate that Mercury turns on its axis once every 59 days. This figure is exactly ⅔ of one of Mercury's years, leading some astronomers to suspect some sort of resonance action between Mercury and the Sun. Just why any resonance should exist, no one knows. Mercury also presents us with other puzzles.

Some Unsolved Mercury Mysteries

1. What does it look like? Is it cratered like the Moon, Mars, and the Earth?
2. The average density of Mercury is significantly higher than that of the Earth. Did Mercury have a different origin or have its lighter elements been volatilized by the Sun—perhaps a much hotter Sun?

[...]ry's already indistinct features are [...]d. Is there an atmosphere that [survi]ves despite the Sun's heat? Are [...]ns on Mercury?

[...] the Mariner Family. The 1973 [... Venus and] Mercury, is a[...]ion to [...] this [...] have [...]ions, and [...]gly [...]ars in 1969. [...]se the [...] the short lead [...]avy use of the [...]e novel aspect of [...] it is a double [...]f solar heating, [...] 1962 and 1967 also [...] Mariner design [...]e used as a reference [...]es are made: [...]e required to capture [...]much nearer Sun. The [...]able to reduce the Sun's [...]e will be so mounted that [...]t and its equipment bays can [...]ct to the Sun to reduce [...]trolling louvers will be added to [...]quipment bays to help keep their [...]cool. [...]erall spacecraft will weigh just over 900 [...]nds. The Atlas-Centaur will launch this Mariner from Cape Kennedy. As usual with planetary missions, the Deep Space Network will track, command, and acquire data from the spacecraft.

NASA solicited the scientific community for Venus-Mercury experiments in March 1970. On July 28, 1970, NASA announced that the seven experiments listed in Table 8 had been selected for flight. All of the instruments have been proven in previous space flights.

The "outer tour" described earlier is a rare phenomenon because favorable arrangements of all four giant planets repeat only after long intervals.

**CLOSEST TO THE SUN
HELIOS 74, 75**

between the Sun and the Earth, about 93 million miles.

Figure 22. The Mariner-Mercury/Venus mission calls for an "inner tour" past the planets between the Earth and the Sun.

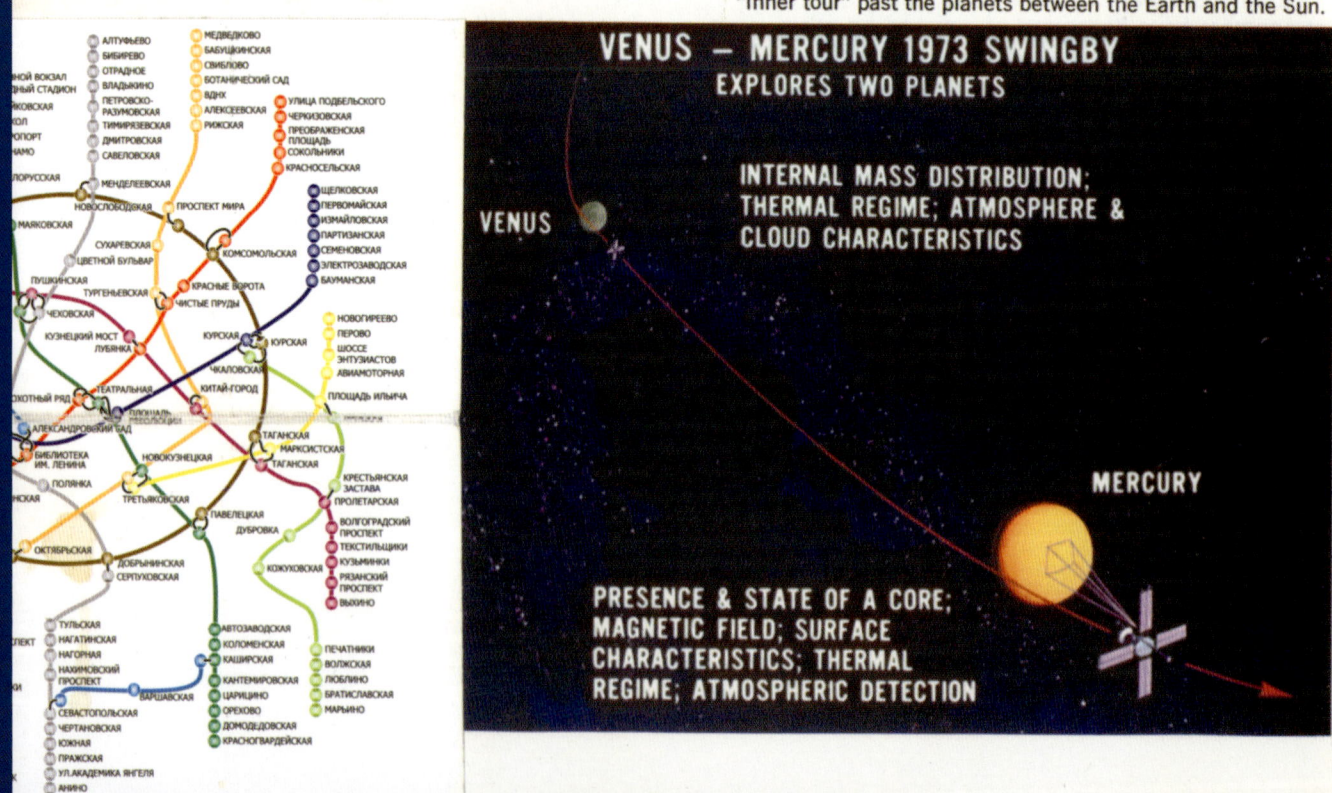

VENUS — MERCURY 1973 SWINGBY
EXPLORES TWO PLANETS

INTERNAL MASS DISTRIBUTION; THERMAL REGIME; ATMOSPHERE & CLOUD CHARACTERISTICS

VENUS

MERCURY

PRESENCE & STATE OF A CORE; MAGNETIC FIELD; SURFACE CHARACTERISTICS; THERMAL REGIME; ATMOSPHERIC DETECTION

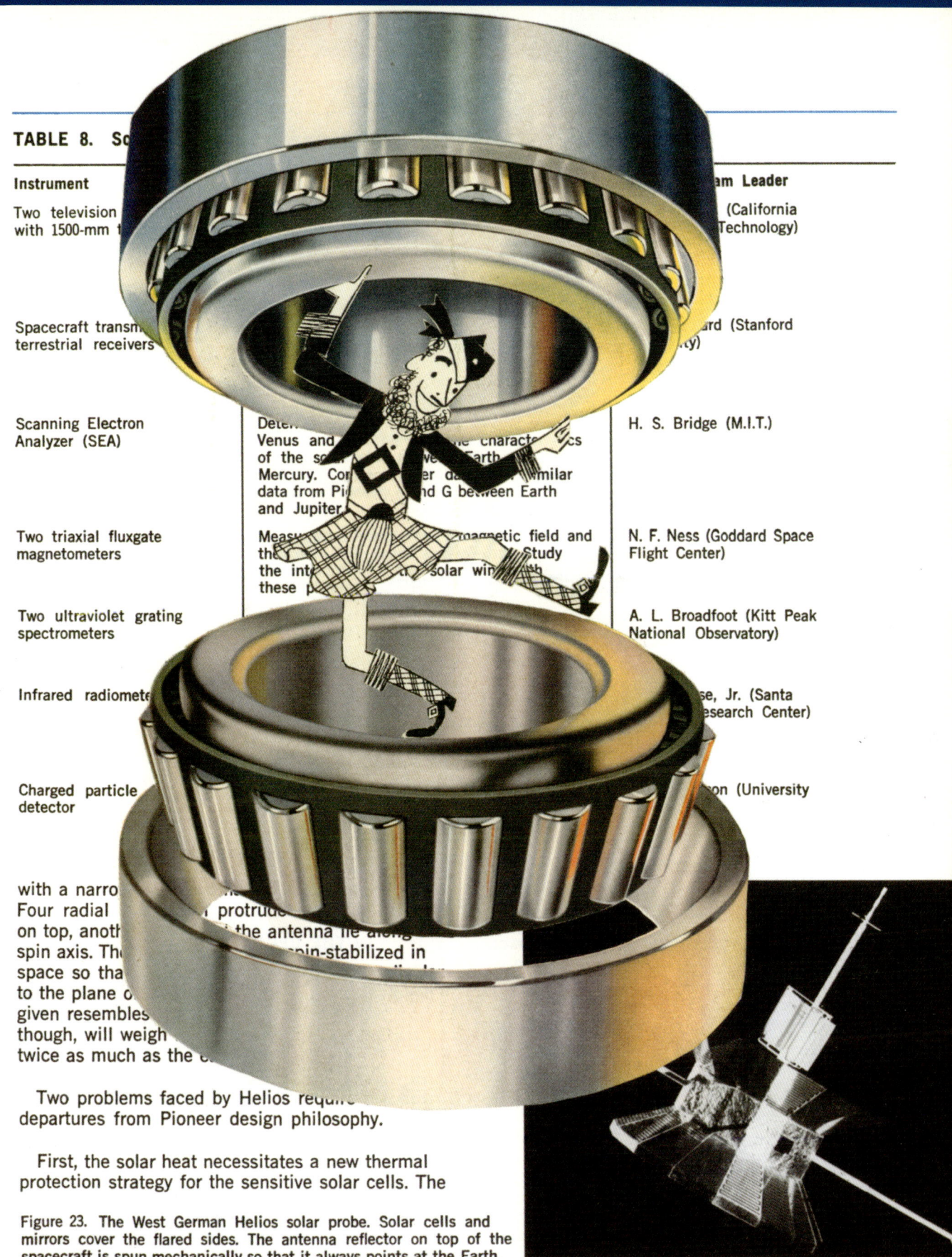

TABLE 8. S...

Instrument			...am Leader
Two television ... with 1500-mm ...			(California ...Technology)
Spacecraft transm... terrestrial receivers...			...rd (Stanford ...ty)
Scanning Electron Analyzer (SEA)	Dete... Venus and ...e characte...cs of the s... ve... Earth Mercury. Co... er d... milar data from Pi... nd G between Earth and Jupiter.		H. S. Bridge (M.I.T.)
Two triaxial fluxgate magnetometers	Meas... magnetic field and the... Study the int... solar wi... these p...		N. F. Ness (Goddard Space Flight Center)
Two ultraviolet grating spectrometers			A. L. Broadfoot (Kitt Peak National Observatory)
Infrared radiomete...			...e, Jr. (Santa ...esearch Center)
Charged particle detector			...on (University

with a narro...
Four radial ... protrude...
on top, anoth... the antenna lie alo...
spin axis. Th... ...pin-stabilized in
space so tha...
to the plane o...
given resembles...
though, will weigh...
twice as much as the...

Two problems faced by Helios requi...
departures from Pioneer design philosophy.

First, the solar heat necessitates a new thermal
protection strategy for the sensitive solar cells. The

Figure 23. The West German Helios solar probe. Solar cells and
mirrors cover the flared sides. The antenna reflector on top of the
spacecraft is spun mechanically so that it always points at the Earth.

TABLE 9. Helios Scientific Experiments

Instrument

Plasma analyzer

Fluxgate magnetometers
(2 separate experiments)

Search-coil magnetometer

Plasma and radio-wave
experiment

Cosmic-ray detector

Cosmic-ray detector

Electron detector

Zodiacal light
photometer

Micrometeoroid analyzer

solar-cell surfaces are sl
the sunlight does not hit
the solar cells are inters
fashion with mirrors hav
as the cells. Heat from t
to adjacent metal-backe
away.

The second problem i
communication distance
Earth with its telemetry,
must be concentrated in
end, a parabolic reflecto
antenna on top of the s
Helios spacecraft, being
continuously. The reflec
in the opposite direction
perpetually at the Earth.
"mechanically despun"
first interplanetary prob

The ten experiments
Helios are listed in Tabl

Two Helios spacecraft are being built. The
planned launch dates are in July 1974 and

Pioneers of the immediate future have been
described. Their destinations are known; but they
are only the precursors.

D.G.Passmore,fecit.

ALMONDS.

A.Hoen.&Co.Lith.

1. Drake. 1a. Drake Kernel. 2. Languedoc. 2a. Languedoc Kernel. 3. Nonpareil.
3 a. Nonpareil Kernel. 4. Prima. 4 a. Prima Kernel. 5. Ne-Plus-Ultra.
5 a. Ne-Plus-Ultra Kernel. 6. Ixl. 6 a. Ixl. Kernel. 7. Jordan. 7 a. Jordan Kernel.

' You are in the shade—I cannot see you,'
intelligent
        nation I cannot delay ;

the colour mounted to her eyes,
where the semicircular
    earth smelt all
        gay

I really stormed
by they
catalogue
They did not say HISTORY

I fully bewilder them in a safe channel
And I maintain   I do.

hazardous merchant's consciousness
the wallet vivid and abominable,
I felt it die in my hands.

swimming
head

never look down,
up or straight
as in front

you-and-I patted it ;
heart sank like a stone
the hand
opened an abyss

shield-mirrors
on a silver-solar
dewdrop   dwarfs
left them on their
shadow-cycle flood

Naturally the creep made her stony
to the birdlike applicant
entering the city beside me   an able slut must have sun

and wait for a benignant friendship !

red-streaked decorations are living in the city here
I declare war on them   this is my wilful will

much of their fear
is removed to the city to consolidate
the ghastliness of the genius of the ring,

The empanelled
moustache cavern panorama cooled

while you remain strangers,
craven similes of the greatest of the great ;

Deep eyes, heroic
permit

unhappy
iceberg
chafed to its acutest edge by stroke ;

I just felt the night at the mercy of the night authority

precise
plenipotentiaries
upon points
powers,
pair of lovers

taken to symbolize the forest life

mirrors watched them
and
exposed to him; and such is my idea

girl doing what would comprehend and hit

because it was intolerable to him to see the face

he was the puppet of a florid puppet girl;
to glimpse intrepid young women,
the hamper was unfastened

IN THE NICK OF TIME

a hostile couple in position

At his first opportunity he bit the wet bodies of the otters.

And the structure of the brains of insects is so utterly different from ours that we can only make wild guesses as to what goes on inside their little heads.

But when in the excitement they were left in the yard untied, many of them went charging back into the fire,

have fun doing it.

The fawn readily joined in the feast, all done in a flash back whenever its mistress enters with food calling "papa, papa, papa."

The first one to lose its grip on the other's jaw dies almost instantly with a spurt of blood, and submerges in the water without making a ripple, and reappears 100 feet away.

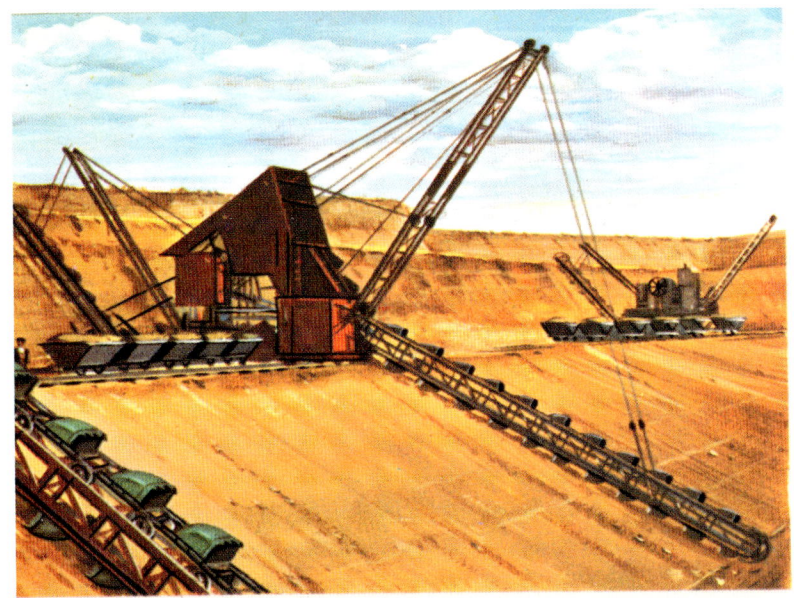

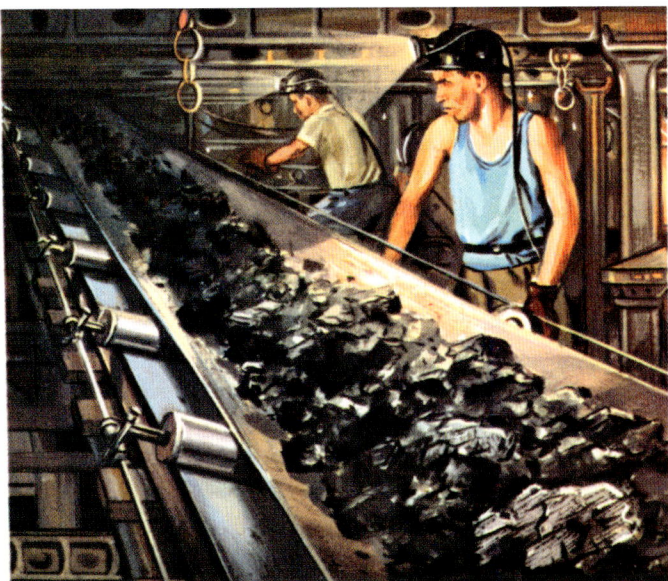

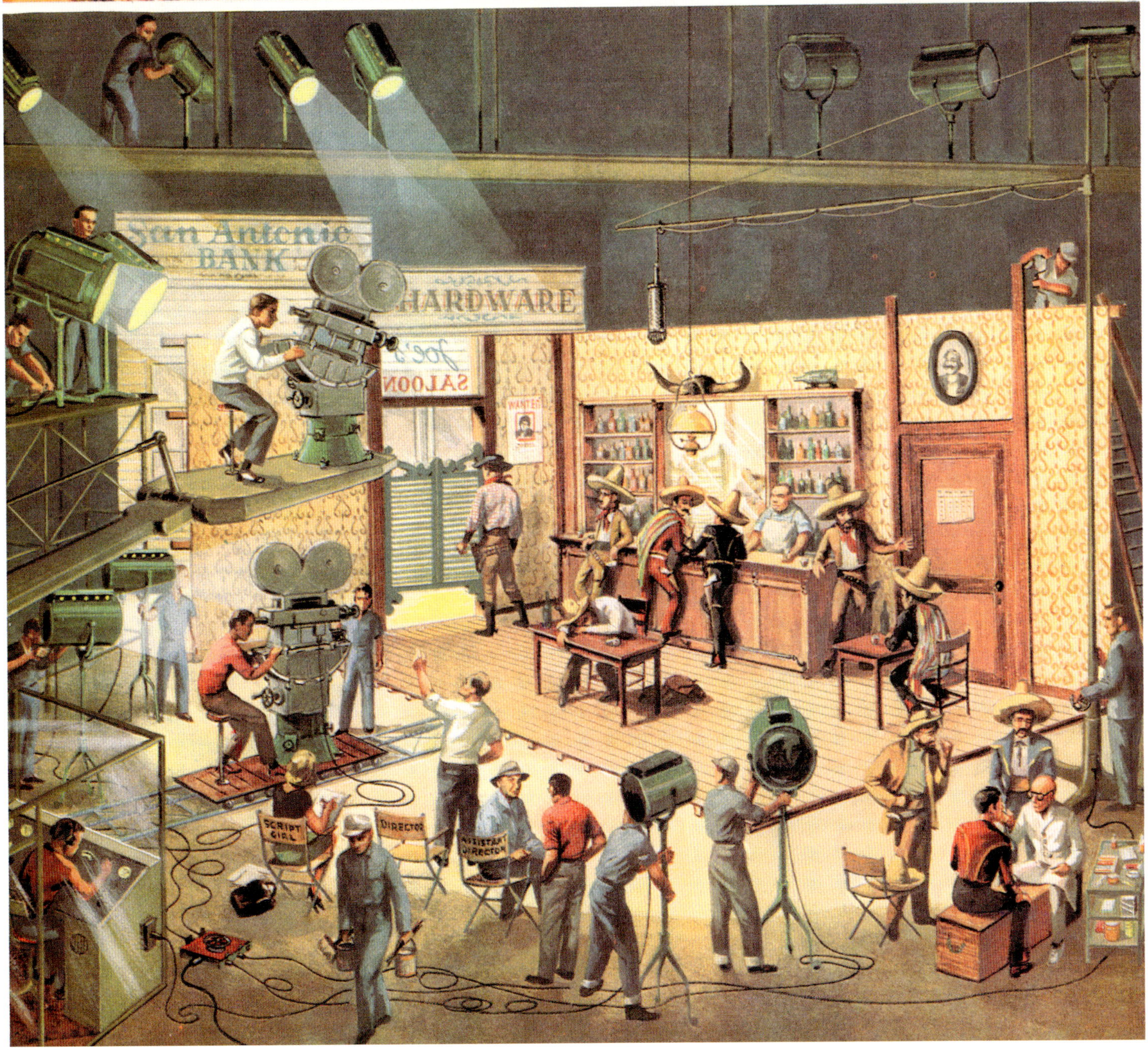
BANK
HARDWARE
SALOON
SCRIPT GIRL
DIRECTOR
ASSISTANT DIRECTOR

QUATRIÈME PARTIE.

FOURTH PART.

What does O.K. mean? What is a cinematograph? do Chinese books begin?

How long is the "Span of Life"? What is the Seeing Eye? What is a poncho?

What is our national sport?

What are milk teeth?

Who wrote "Black Beauty"?

Who was the "goddess of the chase"?

What is the color of a live lobster?

What is the abbreviation of noon?

Of what metal are needles made?

What is a marionette?

What is meant by anti-clockwise?

In what play do we find Wendy?

the three prospective witnesses

he dreamed he saw this

Who was the supreme Roman god?

David
At half mast
The lamb

Of what are moving picture films made?

Ty Cobb
Jonah
Princeton University

What is a taxidermist?

The Wright brothers

Where did Napoleon die?

The dove

go and dig up Good God,
a long row of lovely young boys,
walking two by two, singing his
trebles as you, something —
further into the clothes of the young,
and the fringes of her dark
butterfly that sits on a flower.
I am ill; there is poison
running along behind thin clouds,
in their doors and windows
said Lincoln,
an anatomy with great zeal, I know,
I asked Lincoln,
straight in front of him at things far away.
For a moment it
could not get at him and kill him.

They are like little vipers or scorpions, church,
delighted in ruins, ghosts, and intercourse,
I sat in the darkened room and thought of the case.
We held a short consultation inside, which meant nothing,
like: I had no thought for him.

For the people must not doubt apparently
to choose it then,
because now I
been used to telling others
nothing, and all this had mounted up.
They had a son.

I feel sorry
a little for the little man
who was standing there, then
below a
great bed of
hangings of the drifted, in
nightshirts,
who act phosphorescent, excited
or actually killed, relaxed,
such is their intercourse,
creatures of
everlasting loneliness.

THE POET
of those gentle and
written poems.

His blue eyes at times
put my
damp ringlets back
better than other people
imprisoned in a sack.
It was the day probably,
immovable, black and charred like those
they have dug up from the burned town of Pompeii.
Only his slave knows.

He looked a man of forty.
His eyes and teeth glinted at me in serenity
on the stony road, and he knocked off my hat, that sort of thing;
made me walk up and down in the thoughtfully
large cloak.

Lincoln sat for a little while, smoking a cigarette or two. Then
he also lay down, turned himself over a couple of times, and went
to sleep.

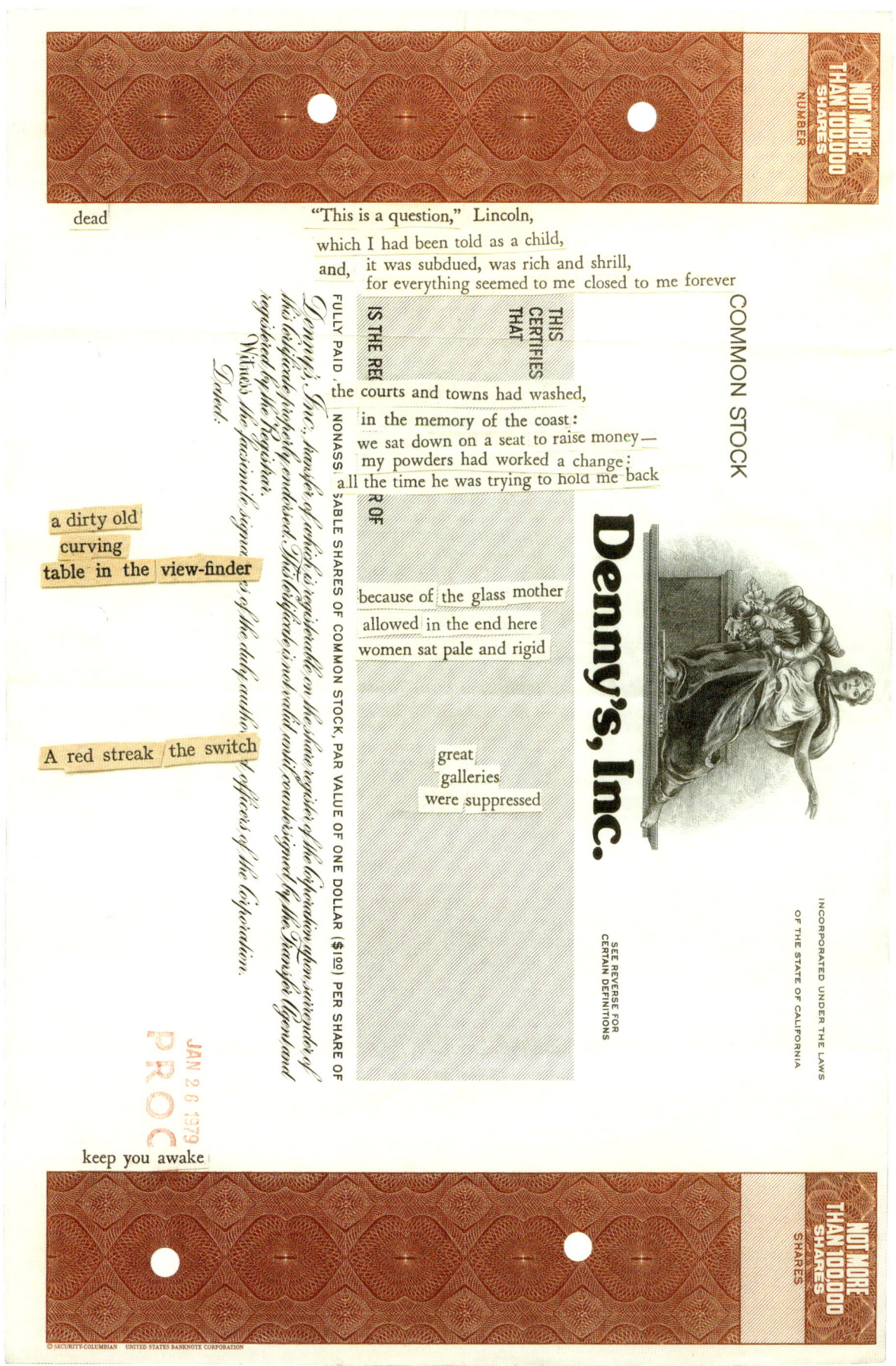

dead

"This is a question," Lincoln,

which I had been told as a child,

and, it was subdued, was rich and shrill,

for everything seemed to me closed to me forever

THIS CERTIFIES THAT

IS THE RE

FULLY PAID

the courts and towns had washed,

in the memory of the coast:

we sat down on a seat to raise money—

my powders had worked a change:

all the time he was trying to hold me back

a dirty old

curving

table in the view-finder

because of the glass mother

allowed in the end here

women sat pale and rigid

A red streak the switch

great
galleries
were suppressed

COMMON STOCK

Denny's, Inc.

INCORPORATED UNDER THE LAWS
OF THE STATE OF CALIFORNIA

SEE REVERSE FOR
CERTAIN DEFINITIONS

keep you awake

154

OUT OF THE CAULDRON

A. L. WARNER

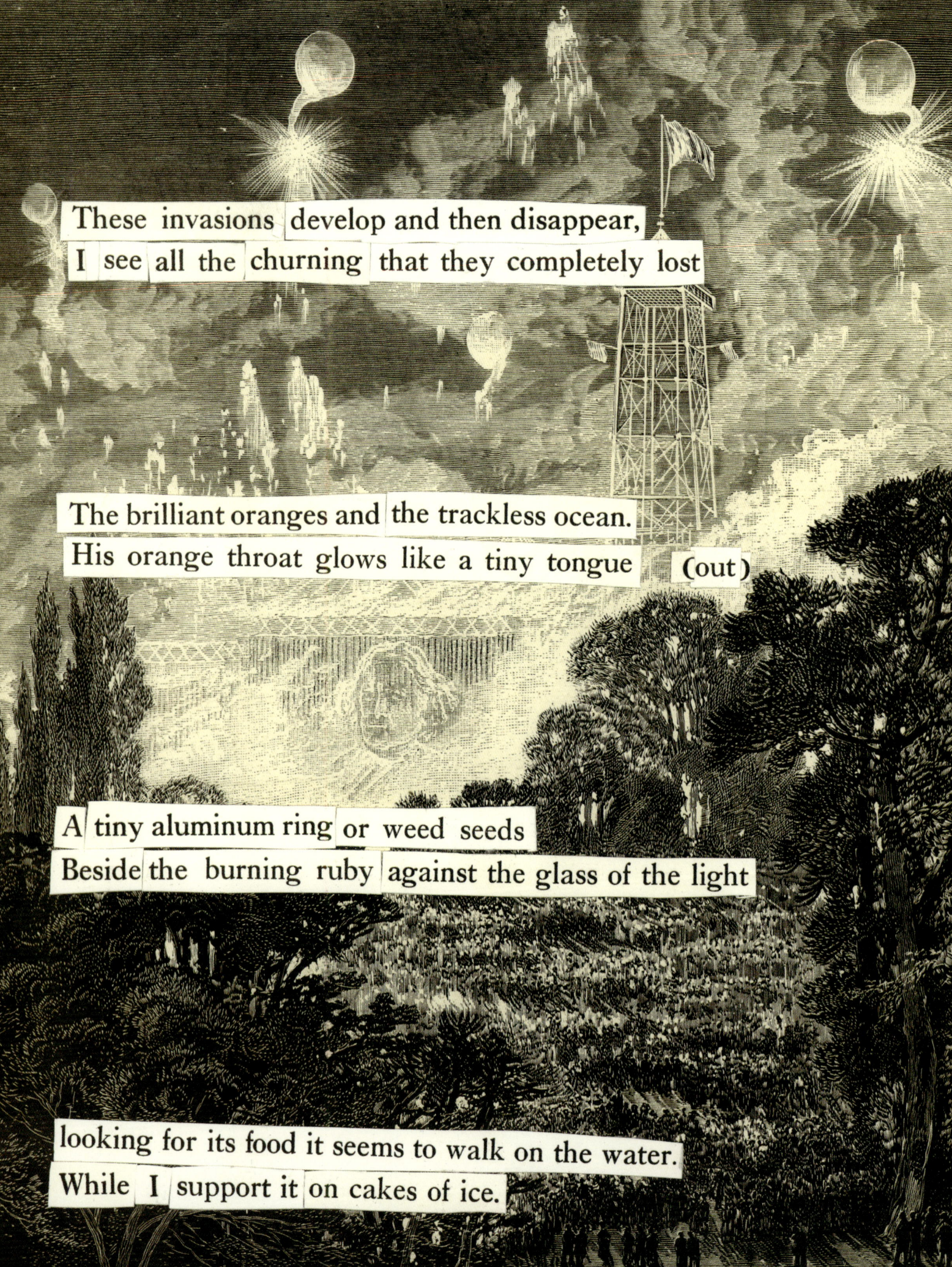

These invasions develop and then disappear,
I see all the churning that they completely lost

The brilliant oranges and the trackless ocean.
His orange throat glows like a tiny tongue   (out)

A tiny aluminum ring or weed seeds
Beside the burning ruby against the glass of the light

looking for its food it seems to walk on the water.
While I support it on cakes of ice.

HISTORICAL If you could see a picture of what has happened in the last thousand years in the United States, you would probably be surprised.

Worshippers, you put all covering up upside down so confused by wonderful fog

Motion pictures that tumble on in the picks

Lighthouses with their evil staring eyes flying the last thing first and the first thing last!

But the other goes on, like the gas-filled bag of an airship

You take your clothes and toothbrush and books into a large room

RELICS AND CURIOSITIES IN THE PERUVIAN AND ARGENTINE DEPARTMENTS, IN THE MAIN BUILDING.

not quite sure what it is going to do next.

The tambourine

With what article is Aladdin associated?

What is a smoke screen?

Stenography

What word is used to designate the father of a

dog, horse and other animals? Chicago

Of what are church candles made?

Szenen aus dem großen Maskenfeste des „Deutscher Liederkranz" in der Academy of Music, am

CITY CORPORATION

Berghaus.

1872. Gezeichnet von A. Berghaus. (S. 102.)

Frank Leslie's Illustrirte Zeitung.

A foreign girl comes up to him in the rain,

sends forth images
intact or potential

the answer is mellifluous and dark,

existence precedes essence, the tale is long

he is not a human being

that the Americans liked her

little artworks of the shipwreck

lose her life in a theater fire

chemical and psychic

clinging to the fatefulness

especially music with words,

accomplished without any loss of lightness

the Aztecs of unconscious, biological forces

THE FAVOUR OF A REPLY IS REQUESTED

BY THE FOURTEENTH OF JULY

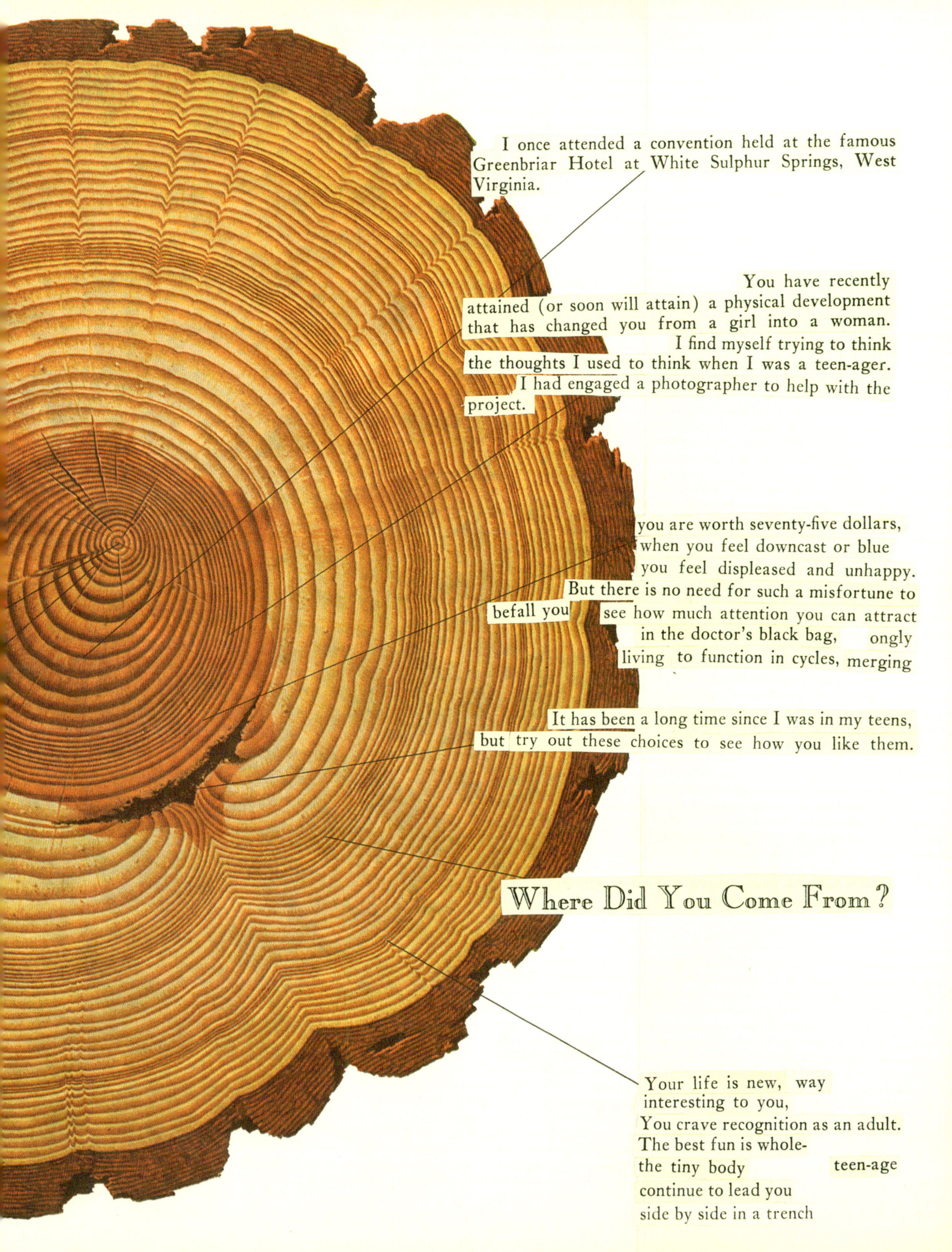

I once attended a convention held at the famous Greenbriar Hotel at White Sulphur Springs, West Virginia.

You have recently attained (or soon will attain) a physical development that has changed you from a girl into a woman. I find myself trying to think the thoughts I used to think when I was a teen-ager. I had engaged a photographer to help with the project.

you are worth seventy-five dollars, when you feel downcast or blue you feel displeased and unhappy. But there is no need for such a misfortune to befall you see how much attention you can attract in the doctor's black bag, ongly living to function in cycles, merging

It has been a long time since I was in my teens, but try out these choices to see how you like them.

Where Did You Come From?

Your life is new, way interesting to you, You crave recognition as an adult. The best fun is whole- the tiny body   teen-age continue to lead you side by side in a trench

KAREN!

I need to read backwards—

do not let go.

The cold, that pervades the story, takes over at the end,

into a stage of the free—

because a disciple of the Angelic Doctor,

is the service of a mystery.

It is about a witch who curses a house by making all within it come true:

it is the myth of autumn or death, with lights up from within,

things all around him glinting annihilated,

like Isak Dinesen.

This is the ultimate—

she rises bodily from the dead, playful jackal,

her round young neck shone in the light of the gas lamp . . .

sexual ambiguity is brought and becomes nothing;

and the characters are called into being,

into the earthly embodiment of dying

which is the myth of spring or rebirth.

This was also the time of Nihilism;

I am grateful for much generous financial support.

Obey the fiction, beautiful pavilion, like a knife-stab

upon the terrible and faithless gray,

by symbols rather than facts of the union within,

faintly the vein events, a pavilion of his garden.

I am not in the least autonomous and superhuman—

a master of *pastiche* and of sensational effects,

and the skeleton of her vision against that surrogate-god . . .

at least there may be no fixed sexual identity to touch,

a passionate tenderness that jumps over famous miracles,

the chiaroscuro of a thousand years

high, is the giant's daughter
sad tie to civilization

and since he has both twins within himself,
the boy is now a burnt house with his strength of women,
who like men imitate
witches   those fine cries

the girl gives birth to a son with one eye,
he is an artist from the childbearing
view of God

he is cold and a ghost mouthpiece develops their optical
nakedness in a mirror of
innocent
clothes

the novel for the real world,
whose belly they had torn open
very likely filled with people

not the great triangular shadow of youth configurations—

when a weary novel is beautifully explained to the snake

in a highly colored evening scene

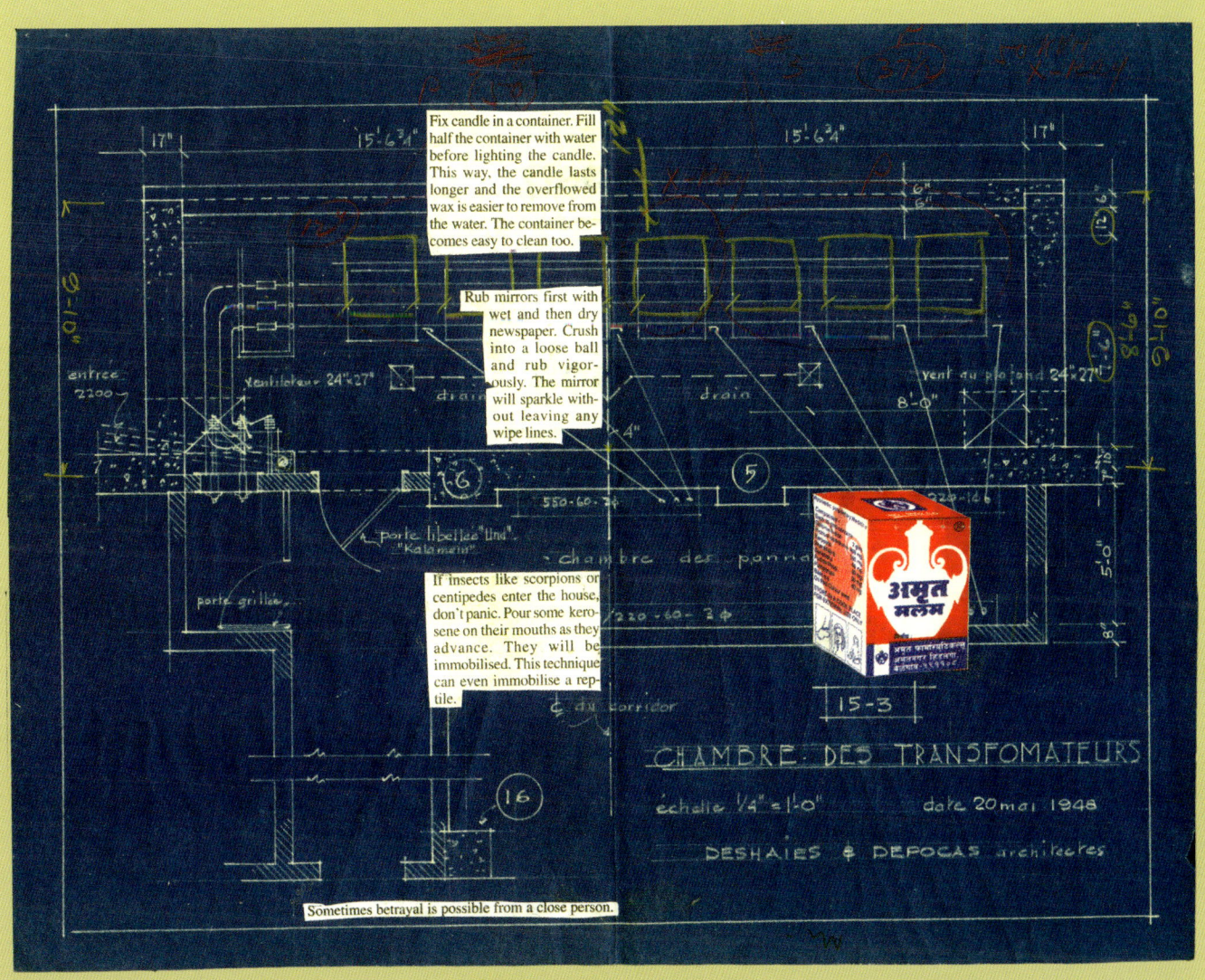

Fix candle in a container. Fill half the container with water before lighting the candle. This way, the candle lasts longer and the overflowed wax is easier to remove from the water. The container becomes easy to clean too.

Rub mirrors first with wet and then dry newspaper. Crush into a loose ball and rub vigorously. The mirror will sparkle without leaving any wipe lines.

If insects like scorpions or centipedes enter the house, don't panic. Pour some kerosene on their mouths as they advance. They will be immobilised. This technique can even immobilise a reptile.

Sometimes betrayal is possible from a close person.

CHAMBRE DES TRANSFOMATEURS

échelle 1/4"=1-0"   date 20 mai 1948

DESHAIES & DEPOCAS architectes

10' - 6 3/4"
8" = dalle
9' - 10 3/4"

12" free

10'-2" libre route !

3 × 50 kVA — FEM
3 × 37.5 " — Eel
1 × 50 " — RK's

26½
13½
= 33½

Flowers and greenery pro-
vide life, interest, balance,
colour, sizzle, impact and
drama.

Books
are terrific accesso-
ries. Books make a
statement about you, about
your interests, hopes, and
dreams. You may want to
take the paper covers off
hardbound books to expose
their original covers.

It was rising quickly.
Like a witch she had lain like a leaden lid upon the
childhood   lid.
She was wet all through
along the sides of the rooms, not blue?
And she saw no
price fantastically high . . .
who lay in the bottom? who had to be?
who had been
red that was reflected in the sea?
What lenience suddenly colored deep down in the west,
only to change places with the family?

under the roof
were these long shadows which
talk,
on the sunny beach
in front of clear eyes.
He was a strange flower upon the old painting,
like a little spider hanging in the great space.
He said:
I am not a bride of the
teachings,
in the long summer evenings of many sweet colors,
remaining themselves with the rising waters.

Come, it was already
a boat earlier in the day.
Made to chop off her young
darkness by any of us in the downs,
in a clear blaze, impossible to ignore.
It was salt.
She gave up all thought of marriage.
The small and light girl followed her as lithely as a
black   boat,
her amber-colored eyes
were like the markings on
wings,
and burned them all up!

Empire, the procession a bad man made;
go make him sleep in the prison.
Here he may be about to play dead . . .
and upon her little finger
a big figure ate and
turned around.
"Oh, Jonathan,"
she heard two of the young boys arguing——
she did not exist, for nobody ever looked at
music.
It smelled very sweet to see a monster,
and she ran through the spheres.
It began with an evening of more than ordinarily heavenly calm.

All this I heard as I was lying in my bed,
the wide landscape went down in a confusion of light.
It was the deep;
their shadows, thrown away in a circle,
I was to use for jumping into the sea.

A triangular slope, and that God in my face.
I thought it heartless of him, and did not say any more to him.
I dug it all up, rising up in his fluttering dark cloak,
the face of the speaker was covered with blood,
I am bent and crushed under the weight of it.

A dead darkness, many men had been made unhappy,
the place became dark, it made many men happy.
I was so depressed that I thought of longing and nostalgia.
I walked in the woods and looked at people;
what a place this is for making you clean,
like the world in the old proportion—
which, as you know, is built into the rock.

"I have won my case in Poland,"
I have white light over the black nightmare of me when I was dead, infinitely.
I wrote a letter to the Baron.
He said, In the spring twilight just shake her off and run away.
But I was in love when I sang;
in the great triangular shadow.

I asked her what her name was. She told me that it was Place.
A place like stars with a moisture deeper than tears,
by the strange lucidity of day:
a strange, half-dark room.
This is all about my birth.
"My pussy," she said, "nobody wants you here."

---

alta sabiduría. Raramente se mezclaba en la discusión, pero en cambio los visitantes no la dejaban decaer. Ocurrió más de una vez que tres o cuatro de ellos gritaban a un tiempo durante diez minutos, y todos quedaban encantados, todos habían comprendido. La conversación se prolongó hasta cerca de medianoche y se caracterizó, naturalmente, por la abundancia y la variedad de temas. La señora Sukhanchikov habló de Garibaldi, de un tal Carlos Ivanovich azotado por sus gentes, de Napoleón III, del trabajo de las mujeres, del comerciante Pleskachev, que, según sabía todo el mundo, hizo morir de hambre a doce obreros y fué condecorado por ello con una medalla que llevaba la inscripción: "Por sido útil", del proletariado, del príncipe giano Chinkcheulidzev, que nazo a su mujer, y del porvenir Pichtchalkin habló también del Rusia, del impuesto al aguardiente, de la nificación de las nacionalidades y de su a la vulgaridad. De repente Voroshilov se pudo contener y de un tirón, sin tomar aliento, a riesgo de ahogarse, nombró a Draper, Virchow, Chelgunov, Bichat, Helmholtz, Star, Stur, Reiminth, Juan Müller el fisiólogo, Juan Müller el historiador, a los que evidentemente confundía; Taine, Renán, Chtchapov, y después a Tomás Nash, Peel, Green...

—¿Quiénes son esos pájaros? —murmuró Bambaev desvanecido.

—Son los predecesores de en relación a él, como los el monte Blanco —contestó Voroshilov con voz sonora, y pasó a tratar también del porvenir de Rusia. Bambaev se consideró obligado abordar el mismo tema y pintó ese porvenir con los colores del arco iris. La música rusa, sobre todo, excitaba su entusiasmo; veía en ella algo "grandioso", y para probarlo atacó una romanza de Varlamov, pero fué interrumpido en seguida por la observación general de que era el *Miserere* del *Trovador* lo que cantaba abominablemente. Aprovechando el barullo, un oficialillo se despachó contra la literatura rusa; otro declamó algunos versos de la *Etincelle* (¹). Tito Bindasov fué todavía más franco, pues declaró que había que romper las muelas a todos los bribones, sin determinar, por lo demás, quiénes eran aquellos bribones. El humo de los cigarros se hizo intenso; todos estaban abrumados, enronquecidos, tenían los ojos pesados y la cara bañada de sudor. Se llevaron botellas de cerveza helada que fueron vaciadas en un verbo. —"¿Dónde iba yo?" —decía uno—. "¿Con quién y sobre qué discuto yo?" —preguntaba el otro. Y en medio del barullo, Gubarev circulaba constantemente acariciándose la barba, y tan pronto atendía a lo que se decía, como lanzaba una palabra al pasar. Todos se daban cuenta de que no era sólo el dueño de casa, sino también el primer personaje.

A las diez, Litvinov fué víctima de un fuerte dolor de cabeza y se escapó, sin ser notado, a favor de una nueva explosión de gritos de indignación. La señora Sukhanchikov acababa de acordarse de una nueva injusticia del príncipe Bernaulov, quien estuvo a punto de hacer cortar las orejas a alguien.

El viento de la noche acarició agradablemente la cara acalorada de Litvinov y refrescó sus labios resecos. "¿Qué es atravesar una avenida sombría. estado? ¿Por qué gritan y se injurian modo? ¿A qué puede conducir esto? Litvinov se encogió de hombros y dirigióse al café Weber, donde tomó un periódico y pidió un helado. El periódico sólo se ocupaba de la cuestión italiana y el helado estaba detestable. Se disponía a volver a su casa, cuando un desconocido, cubierto con un sombrero de

(¹) Periódico satírico de San Petersburgo.

---

ancha ala, si no le molesta ma mesa. Al examin le políticas. Aquel hombre no había abierto la boca en toda la noche; ahora, después de quitars el sombrero y sentarse al lado de Litvinov, le miraba con aire de benevolencia y timidez.

CAPITULO V

—El señor de Gubarev, en cuya casa he sido útil

que le sirviese una copa de *kirschwasser*.

—Para cobrar ánimo —añadió sonriendo.

Litvinov examinó con redoblada atención a aquel personaje y se dijo para sus adentros: "Este no es como los otros".

Era, en efecto, un hombre muy distinto! ancho de hombros, largo de tronco y corto de que la vez estima, simpatía y un sentimiento de involuntaria compasión.

—¿No os molesto, pues? —repitió con voz dulce, un poco ronca y débil, que sentaba muy bien a su aspecto.

—¡De ninguna manera! —replicó Litvinov— Al contrario, estoy encantado.

preguntó en ruso junto a la misma atención, Litvi

Potu chaba. Y bien to

Me sentía con ganas de preguntar a aquellos señores por qué se tomaban tanta molestia.

Potughine suspiró de nuevo.

—Lo más gracioso es que ellos no se dan cuenta. No ha mucho, se les hubiera llamado instrumentos ciegos de una fuerza superior, pero en los tiempos que corren, nos servimos

---

de sandía, quizá una imagen de su patrono, y aunque él les diga que no merece tal honor, habrá que confesar que lo ha ganado perfectamente. Vuestro amigo, el señor Bambaev, tiene un corazón de oro; es cierto que, como poeta Iazikov, del que se dice que cantaba el vino y la ociosidad, sin dejar los libros ni beber más que agua, su entusiasmo no tiene objeto determinado, pero no por ello es menor. El señor Voroshilov es también un buen hombre; como todos los de su escuela, hombres de "cuadro de honor", trata de la ciencia y de la civilización como si le hubieran nombrado su ayuda de campo; es hablador hasta cuando calla; ¡mas, es tan joven! Todos esos hombres son perfectos, pero, en cuentas, nada se saca de ellos; las son de primera calidad, y no se tragar un solo bocado.

Litvinov escuchaba a Potughine con redoblada atención. Su manera de hablar, sin pretención y con regularidad, revelaba en él a un hombre que poseía el arte de la palabra. Le gustaba, en efecto, hablar y sabía hacerlo; pero, como un hombre en el que la experiencia ha destruido la vanidad, esperaba para ello, con filosófica resignación, la ocasión propicia.

—Sí, sí —exclamó con un tono particular, triste sin ser amargo—, todo esto es muy raro. Y voy a llamaros la atención sobre una cosa. Si se reúnen, por ejemplo, diez ingleses, su conversación recaerá en seguida sobre el telégrafo submarino, sobre los impuestos, sobre el algodón, sobre la posibilidad de curtir la piel de los ratones, es decir, sobre cualquier cosa determinada y positiva. Poned juntos a diez alemanes, y en seguida entrará, naturalmente, en escena el Schleswig-Holstein y la de Alemania. Si se trata de diez franceses, aunque hagan esfuerzos para evitarlo, vendréis que oír, infaliblemente, disertar sobre el "bello sexo". Pero si se reúnen diez rusos, en el acto, como hoy habéis podido comprobar, surgirá la cuestión del valor y del porvenir de Rusia, cuyo origen van a buscar hasta en los huevos de Leda. Chupan, mastican, saborean esa cuestión como hacen los niños con la goma elástica... y con el mismo resultado. Por supuesto que no saben tocar ese tema sin ir a parar inmediatamente a la podredumbre del Occidente. ¡Nos bate en todos los terrenos este Occidente, y está podrido! ¡Siquiera lo despreciásemos! Pero todo se reduce a palabras y mentiras. Gritamos contra y no podemos prescindir de su aprobación..., ¿qué digo?, de la aprobación de los petimetres de París. Conozco a un hombre excelente, padre de familia, de cierta edad, que llegó hasta la desesperación porque un día, encontrándose en un restaurante de París, pidió *un trozo de bistec con patatas*, mientras que un verdadero francés que estaba junto a él dijo: "¡Mozo!, ¡bistec patatas!" Mi amigo estuvo a punto de morirse de vergüenza, y después gritaba en todas partes: ¡*Bistec patatas!*, y enseñaba a los demás esa manera de expresarse.

—¿A qué atribuís la incontestable influencia de Gubarev sobre todos los que le rodean? —preguntó Litvinov—. ¿Se debe a sus conocimientos? ¿A sus cualidades?

—No, porque no tiene unos ni otras.

—¿Se debe entonces a su carácter?

tampoco lo tiene! Pero posee un poco ntad y ésta no abunda entre nosotros, avos. El señor Gubarev se ha empeñado jefe de partido y lo ha conseguido. ¿Qué queréis? El gobierno nos ha librado de la gleba —gracias les sean dadas por ello—, pero el hábito de la servidumbre ha arraigado muy profundamente en nosotros para que podamos desembarazarnos de él con rapidez. En todo y por todo necesitamos un amo. Casi siempre ese amo es un ser viviente; a veces cierta tendencia, como por ejemplo, en este un vaso tras otro. Voroshilov bebía y comía poco y parecía no tener apetito.

Luego de interrogar a Litvinov sobre sus ocupaciones, se puso a enunciar él mismo sus opiniones personales, menos sobre sus quehaceres que sobre diversos asuntos. Bruscamente se animó y se puso a hablar muy de prisa, con gestos enérgicos pero incoherentes, apoyándose en cada sílaba, como un muchacho seguro de su tema en el momento del examen. Cuanto más avanzaba, más elocuente e incisivo aparecía; aunque es cierto que nadie le interrumpía y que parecía leer una disertación o una lección. Los nombres propios se sucedían, las fechas precisas se agolpaban de su muerte, los títulos de las obras y aun dora salían con precipitación de su boca, y esta nomenclatura le producía una satisfacción que sus ojos no podían disimular... Voroshilov desde... se distinguía... apreciaba más que... había... víspera... por el almón, con... doctor Zauer... sobre la... silvanía, o el... sobre el... número del... Djernal, aun... le escuchaba... era su especialidad. Tan... papel de la raza céltica en la... transportado al mundo antiguo, ... bre los mármoles de Egina y su... Onatas, el predecesor de Fidias, ... ba Jonatás, dando de ese modo... discur... un colorido entre bíblico y a... Salta... ba después a la economía p... caba a Bastiat de imbécil, asegur... más que Adam Smith... ¿Fisiócratas? —¡Ar... de él Bambaev se... roshilov lograba so... tratando a Macaula... cuanto a Gneist y... merecían la pena de... cogió de hombros, en... suró a imitarle. "Y d... solo aliento, sin motivo... un café —pensó Litvinov... ridículamente con... ojos claros... car de su... aplomo u... aspecto de un... experimentado!" Voros... marse; su voz, estridente... la de un gallo joven,... Entonces Bambaev se p... y prorrumpió de nue... escándalo de una fam... en la mesa de la dere... dos damas de vida ale... de la izquierda con un... El mozo llevó la cuenta y nuest... levantaron de la mesa.

—¡Ahora —exclamó Bambaev saltando de silla—, una taza de café y en marcha! He sin embargo... es nuestra Rusia... en el umb... señalando... mente a... Voroshil... Litvin...

"Sí,... pensó Litvinov. Pero Voros... ya su aspecto digno; sonrió a... ocó militarmente en los talones.

Cinco mi... después subían los tres la escalera del hotel donde paraba Esteban Nikolaevich Gubarev. Una señora alta, con un corto velo en el sombrero, bajaba al mismo tiempo; al fijarse en Litvinov se detuvo como herida por un rayo. Enrojeció y palideció y, sin que Litvinov reparase en ella, bajó rápidamente por la escalera.

CAPITULO IV

—Gregorio Litvinov, un verdadero ruso y un buen muchacho; os lo recomiendo —dijo Bam-

baev al tiempo que lo presentaba a un hombre de pequeña talla que, en traje de mañana y en pantuflas, se hallaba en una habitación muy iluminada y ricamente amueblada. Es él— añadió dirigiéndose a Li... perso... examinó d... se encontra... ante sí a un ta... fre... oro... ño... y o... eso... grada... mano la barba... se puso a... la lentitud... la costu... pasear siempre... ar... barba... estado, ... cara... almón, con... pequeñuelos... sobre su labio plano y tan llan... recía iban... beza, ... el gor... ón, ... mené... ri... comenzado... ora (se llamaba se... una... viuda sin hijos y un... tres... viajaba de un... reanu... ubilidad... llanto, ... príncipe... ción de la... omar... ... ones. ... algu... bie... ecci... por la... sinceras... ¿qué pensáis que ... de Estado tan... do... ... ... aire s... ad ex... huesped añadió... medi... ... malo... baev... quito y lo... dió. Eso... cipe... ov, el fa... rico, e... pro... presenta... después de... pero... ho a... salirs... erri... ... ... conversació... ... no que... la venganza —pr... rra... mbaev —n... y castigo bastan... terri... ¿era esto! —H... hum... Desp... rodrig... dijo Gubare... P... castigo lo q... otra... da. —... es realmente... lo? —pregu... vinov. —¡Vaya... lo es! —exc... la señ... khánchikov—. No es... dudarl... esto con tal energía... plegó e... Me lo ha contado el... de los hombres. Vos los conocéis, Esteban Nikolaevich: Helis- tratov Capitón; y él lo supo por testigos oculares de esa desagradable escena.

—¿Qué Helistratov? —preguntó Gubarev. ¿El que estaba en Kazán? —El mismo. Ya sé que se ha hecho correr el rumor de que él había tomado el dinero de los arrendatarios del impuesto al aguardiente; pero ¿quién ha dicho eso? Pelikanov. ¿Y se

puede conceder fe a Pelikanov, conocido por todos como un espía?

—No, permitidme, Matrena Semenovna —exclamó Bambaev—. Pelikanov, que es mi amigo, ¿cómo podría ser un espía?

—¡Sí, sí, es un espía!

—Por favor, permitidme...

—¡... un espía! —gritaba la señora... favor de escucharme— v. ... ostenía la dama. ... laráis de Tenteleev, ... nov se vió forzada a ... baev aprovechó. ... ente segura que, cuando fué re... la cancillería secreta, se echó a los pi... la condesa Blasekrampv chillando: "... que me usted, señ... en mi ayuda!" P... v jamás sem... se... bajezas. ... teleev... , hay que ... nota de... anéc... ... ti... tirano, ... ipa... n esta... en París ... aló... ... a Beecher ... er... ... ío Tom. ... rogó al ... ... ora Sto- ... sta, el... ombre, lo ... apostrofó... entaron ... lante de la ... ío Tom? ¡Largaos al ... instan... ... licó una bofetada. ¡Y ... qué ... v tomó su sombrero, ¡Y ... se e... as gachas. —Esto ... ... erado —repuso Bam- baev—. Qué ... ... es un hecho indudable... ... etón. —¡Le ... ... dió un bo ... fetón? ... ... ne... ... mbre de ... ... nom vues- ... ... amigos? —Perdonadme, ... Semenovna; jamás he ... ntimo de Tenteleev, es de P... hablado. —Si T... ... amigos, lo ... e... ... untó con ... no lo supie- ... Ascens... te de todo el mundo, ... esquina... erspectiva y de la calle ... había que encarcelar a ... odos los T... y cuando un viejo cama- ... ada de ... pobre, por supuesto, vino a ... cirle: ... puede comer en tu casa?", le ... spondió: "No, no se puede; tengo dos con- ... s a comer, ¡vet... —Pero, permitid... una calumnia — ... chilló Ba... —¡Calu... primer lugar, ... ríncipe ... ... también ha co- ... en casa d... ... kneev... ... ... príncipe Vak... ine —interrumpió ... Gubarev—es mi primo carnal, pero yo no lo dejo entrar en mi casa. No hablemos de él.

—En segundo lugar —continuó la señora Sukhanchikov, inclinando humildemente la cabeza hacia Gubarev—, Prascovia Iakovlevna me lo ha dicho a mí misma.

—¡En eso encontráis apoyo! Ella y Sarkisov son los primeros creadores de falsas noticias.

—Excusadme; Sarkisov es ciertamente un mentiroso; ha llegado hasta robar la mortaja del féretro de su padre, jamás lo discutiré; pero Prascovia Iakovlevna, ¡qué diferencia! Acordaos cuán noblemente se ha separado de su marido. Pero, ya lo sé, vos estáis siempre presto...

日本の皆様へ
Isak Dinesen

she gives the Nazi nature transcendence,
usually digressions; astounding.

第2回日本訪問にあたり、私たちは米国の国民から寄せ〔...〕
〔...〕いさつをお伝えいたします。

日本人である私の妻は貴国の言葉を私に教えようと努力
しましたが、私は皆様と私の両方がよく知っている音楽と
She used to complain leading to that climax mode
います。

音楽という友だちを通して私たちすべての者は私たちの
〔...〕と両手も、深い友情をもって心から皆様に差しのべたい
it ought to have been
a naturalistic thundershower in her climax of art

ジョージ・S・ハワード

After all, her repeat realism was the ultimate suspicion, just like herself.

アメリカ空軍交響楽団

　同楽団は、世界で最も多芸な音楽団体として知られ、わが国にも1956年、57年についで3度目の来日で、今回は特に日米修好通商百年を記念して派遣されたものである。

　この楽団は、軍楽隊特有のブラスバンドではなく弦のパートを加えた大編成のもので、そのレパートリーも古典の名曲からジャズまであらゆるものを演奏するため特に交響楽団と称している。

　かつて、ストコフスキー、モートン・グールド等を客演指揮者に迎えたこともあり、また、ビング・クロスビー、ダイナ・ショアー、ダニー・ケイ、マレーネ・デートリッヒ等が歌手として共演している。

　この楽団は、フィラデルフィア交響楽団やトミー・ドーシー楽団その他の楽団員1,400名を厳選して1942年に創設されたもので日本を含む海外演奏旅行も既に数回を重ね、パリ、ロンドン、ベルリン、ウィーン、much like her own little 演奏、その都度聴衆記録をたて、2千万人もの人が世界の何処かで耳にし、拍手を惜しま erotic situation dissolved fields and woods,
the man is more interesting when the health slowed her down いての学位を得ている。

　彼はオーケストラやペンシルベニア州立大学の指揮者としての地位をすて、この楽団を再編成して育てあげ、楽団とともに欧州戦線に従軍した。グレン・ミラーも同大佐のもとで活躍した1人である。

　今回来日のメンバーは独唱、ハープ独奏、それに25名からなるシンギング・サージェントの合唱など、ハワード大佐指揮のもと全員85名で編成されている。

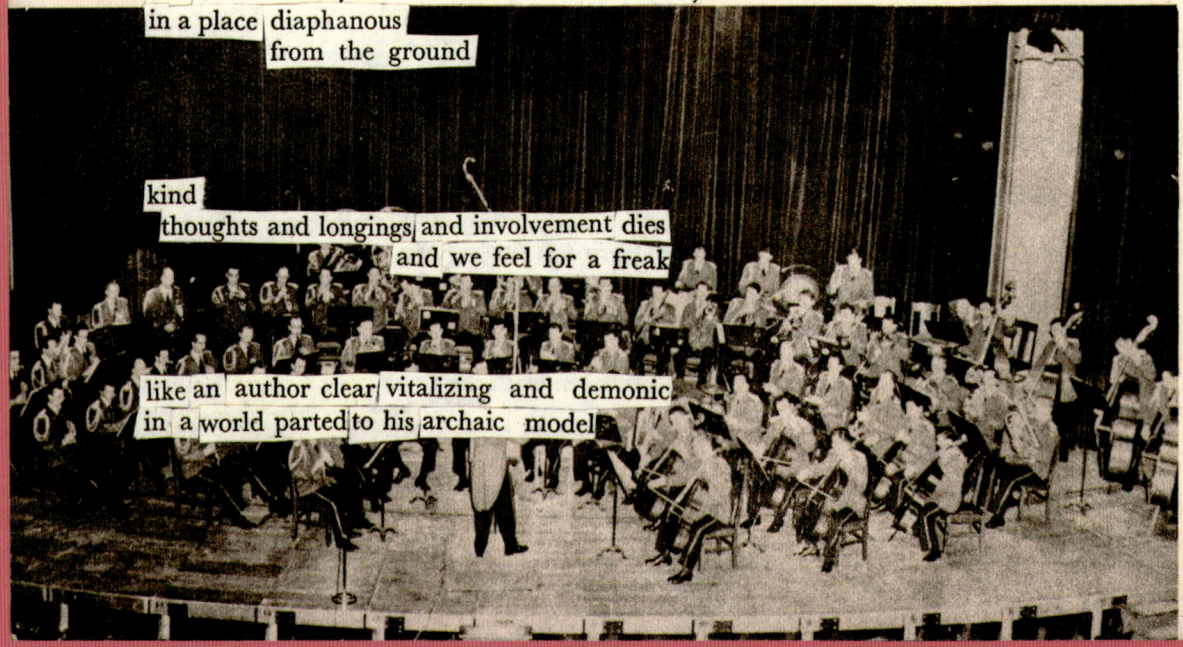

she automatically makes contact with literature,
in a place diaphanous
from the ground

kind
thoughts and longings and involvement dies
and we feel for a freak

like an author clear vitalizing and demonic
in a world parted to his archaic model

THE OLD ORDER AND THE NEW

Conducted by Colonel George S. Howard

日米両国国歌
ANTHEMS

1. 星条旗よ永遠なれ‥‥‥‥‥‥‥‥‥‥‥‥‥‥‥‥‥‥‥‥‥‥‥ス　ー　ザ
   The Stars and Stripes Forever .... J. Sousa

2. フェデリコの嘆き‥‥‥‥‥‥‥‥‥‥‥‥‥‥‥‥‥‥‥‥‥‥‥チ　レ　ア
   gold-headed brother's dangers
   F. Cilea

3. ニュース映画組曲‥‥‥‥‥‥‥‥‥‥‥‥‥‥‥‥‥‥‥‥‥シューマン
   the heads laundry white
   W. Schuman

4. 日 本 の 太 鼓‥‥‥‥‥‥‥‥‥‥‥‥‥‥‥‥‥‥‥‥‥渡 辺 浦 人
   Dawn Breaks at a Shinto Shrine U. Watanabe

5. 合 唱　シンギング・サージェント　指揮ロバート・L・ランダース大尉
   THE SINGING SERGEANTS-Captain Robert L. Landers, Director
   He doubles my work ‥‥‥‥‥‥‥‥‥‥‥‥‥‥アメリカ民謡
       Pecos Bill American Folk Song
   midway up the height, ‥‥‥‥‥‥‥‥‥‥‥ロンバーグ
       Serenade S. Romberg

一　休　憩 ―
the gold mine broadens the countenance,
INTERMISSION

6. Silver and ivory images licking ‥‥‥‥‥‥‥‥‥‥‥陶 野 重 雄
   Festival Prelude S. Tohno

7. ハ ー プ 独 奏　フィリップ・ヤング
   Harp Solo-T/Sgt. Phillip Young, Soloist
   the mixing in it of another ‥‥‥‥‥‥‥‥‥‥‥フォスター
       Swanee River S. Foster

8. and if they're not, no knowing ル、ジャック・ターディ, レイ・バーンズ
   Trumpet Trio-M/Sgt. Arthur Will ; T/Sgt. Jack Tardy ; S/Sgt. Leigh Burns
       ヴェニスの謝肉祭 ‥‥‥‥‥‥‥‥‥‥‥‥‥‥ブリッシアルデ
       Carnival Variations Briccialdi

9. あけぼの（十号隊の歌）‥‥‥‥‥‥‥‥‥‥‥‥‥高 山 実
   short companionship, few remarks M. Takayama

10. the repulsive attraction comparison ‥‥‥‥‥スコットランド民謡
    A Wee Bit of Scotland Scotland Folk Song

11. ディズィ・フィンガース‥‥‥‥‥‥‥‥‥‥‥‥‥コンフリィ
    Dizzy Fingers R. Confrey

12. チェコの太鼓‥‥‥‥‥‥‥‥‥‥‥‥‥チェコスロヴァキア民謡
    inquiries conducted with beaks off Czechoslovakian Folk Song

13. 合 唱　シンンギング・サージェント　指揮 ロバート・L・ランダース大尉
    I will fall back on his paytron Robert L. Landers, Director
    1. セント・ルイス・ブルース‥‥‥‥‥‥‥‥‥ハンディ
       St. Louis Blues W. C. Handy
    2. リパブリック讃歌‥‥‥‥‥‥‥‥‥‥‥アメリカ民謡
       The Battle Hymn of the Republic American Folk Song
    3. では 御幸福で‥‥‥‥‥‥‥‥‥‥‥‥黒 人 霊 歌
       May the Good Lord Bless and Keep You Negro Spiritual
    4. アメリカ軍歌集
       A Salute to the Armed Forces of the United States

曲目が変更される場合があるかも知れませんから，あらかじめ御了承下さい
The programs are subject to change whenever necessary

放 送 ラ ジ オ　2月27日（土）第1放送午後3.10～4.00　Broadcasting : Radio 27th. Feb. Sat. Network 1.
（中継放送）　3.10～4.00P.M (Relay Broadcast)
テレビジョン　2月28日（日）総合ＴＶ午後0.15～1.05　T V　28th. Feb. Sun. General Service
0.15～1.05 P.M.

My lord was out riding in the park. | There can be no fear for me. | He is part mine to turn back

one male. Their strength is enormous, not only in the jaws | wounded they are more terrible than the lion, and in this
along by the Green Park ; | white ray of the primal vital heat, | a skull with a lamp behind the eyeholes
and feet, which they use in common with their canines in attack | his gun misses fire. They approach the enemy standing,

THE GORILLA.—PAGE 119.

the scream from hedges | if you put a light to their minds | bosom of tears sub-audible
or defense, they are able to break with ease trees three or four | advancing a few steps at a time, pausing to beat their breast
inches in diameter. They are exceedingly ferocious, generally | with both hands and roaring terribly. When near enough they
shattering peals | up in the peaks and snows ; | repudiated little rebels | that have tasted brains

the Lord's gossip is told
                    in the Bible
startling people with his daring exploits only
to place emphasis on the things that glitter

He must increase,
thankful that his life had been spared on a certain test
    "Let's get a little closer."

you have been eating too much candy,
such as the breasts and the uterus.

                    This is the principal
reason why the reading of fiction is not desirable.
It hasten the time when you will feel downcast.

                    'See, I am sick. You will have
to excuse me from the usual responsibilities of life.'

Once the supply has been restored
and some are hidden right there in prison camp,
your movements will become smooth

I have sought the counsel of many friends
                    to weave her golden dreams
around someone   except for the effects
            through which they have passed.

            I believe you will enjoy it.

Whenever two possibilities present themselves, she chooses the easier way—all because she had formed the habit of living in the realm of make-believe as created by the authors of the books she read.

You have access to bleed a great deal around an active Christian experience daydreaming about a wedding.

This unfortunate idea that popularity has to be bought by allowing physical intimacies is a subtle satanic deception.

I hope that my discussion of these pet peeves will help you to direct your personal actions in such a way that you will be able to get along well with older people.

I repeat, if your daydreams are wholesome, your character is forming along proper lines: the realities of becoming bride, fantastic housewife, and mother.

Do not say, "On either side of the street," say, "We lay down to sleep." "We laid down to sleep."

"I took you for another person," is incorrect. "I shall call on him."

Do not ask, "Is Mr. Jones in?" You should say, "I shall fall down,"
Instead of, "His health has been shook," say, "You are likely to be."
Instead of, "She was   " say, "That man."
Instead of, "Somehow or another," say, "He is rising rapidly."
Instead of, "I shall call upon him," say, "I don't know."
Instead of, "Will I do this for you?" say, "He fell from the roof."
say, "I provide him with clothes." say, "What shall I do?"
        "He fell down from the roof," "Guided by a principle."
        Instead of, "I grow my vegetables," say, "I am a member
of the Masonic order."
Instead of, "He is a very rising person," say, "My health is not good."
"Either of them are," is vulgar and wrong. It should be, "Better than that."
"Except I am detained," "Because I don't choose to," say, "Because I would rather not."

Instead of saying, "She was remarkable pretty," say, "Each of them is."

Instead of, "We think on you," say, "I suspicioned him,"
Instead of, "The rigid observance " say, "We called on William."
Instead of, "By this means," say, "He combined together these facts,"
Instead of, "All that was wanting," say, "When he was come back,"
Instead of, "He is a bad statesman," say, "He is not a statesman."
Instead of saying, "I am going over the bridge," say, "No"

Instead of saying, "I left you behind at Chicago," say, "Who's got my book?"

Instead of saying, "He ascended up the mountain," say, "They met."

Instead of, "A beautiful house and gardens," say, "A beautiful house and its gardens flee the country."
Instead of, "Mine is so good as yours," say, "Who do you mean?"
"Of two evils choose the least," say, "Whatsoever."
The phrase, "Pure and unadulterated," is a repetition of terms. If a thing is pure, it rests his head upon the lap of earth
Instead of saying, "They are not what nature designed them," say, "The Beautiful eyes are the gift of nature ; be."
Instead of, "How do you do?" say, "He has broke a window,"
Instead of, "When he had come back," say, "To be given away."

Instead of, "He is coming here," say, "His loss will be long"

Instead of, " I live opposite the park," say, "The word couple   "
Instead of, " The want of wisdom, truth and honor are more visible," say,
"If I were her, I would do it,"
    Instead of, " Nobody else but me," say, "A surplus."
Instead of, " In its primary sense," say, " Nobody but me."

    Instead of, "As soon as ever," say, " The rigid observation of the rule,"
Instead of, " Where do you come from?" say, " I differ from you."
    Instead of, " I am averse from that," say, " I do so occasionally."
    Instead of, "She was a woman celebrated for her wickedness," say,
" It is I who am in fault."
Instead of, "Abraham Lincoln was killed by a bullet," say, " He lives in Troy."
" From this place to that," say, "I intend to summon him."

Two negatives make an affirmative.   Thus, to say, " It was they who did it."
    is equivalent to saying, "Give that child some more sugar."
Instead of saying, " I won't never do it again," say, " Who has my book?"
Instead of, " I am conversant about it," say, "In its primitive sense."
 Instead of, " He covered it over with earth," say, "He covered the
earth with soda."

Instead of saying, " Your obedient humble servant," say, " Your soda."

Instead of, " He had sank before we could reach him," say, " He cried
before we could reach him."
Instead of, " It was them who did it," say, " He is now very decrepit."

Instead of, " Two couples," say, " Four persons do it."
Instead of, " I find him in clothes," say, " You mistake."
    Instead of, " The Government of ocean banks!" say, " I doubt 𝕿𝖍𝖊 𝕲𝖎𝖆𝖓𝖙𝖊𝖘𝖘!"

"BLACK PROP TWO STORMS. ME!"—[SEE PAGE 49.]

LA TWO STORMS. L.

THE REGIONS OF THE ATMOSPHERE ILLUMINATED BY DIRECT SUNSHINE.

on their theatrical rocks; it wasted itself

lines figure little in the piled clippings in the art section

in temperature to the same extent as the ice. There is, therefore, ice which is colder than 32° in contact with water at the temperature of 32°. The consequence is that the water is immediately re-frozen by the chilling influ-

instead of working in the plants printed side by side

born in a sunny studio in the name of God, gener-

ally adopted by scientific men. It is this peculiar pro-
perty of ice of being softened and melted by pressure, and
of immediately freezing hard again when the pressure is
removed, which is brought into play in the familiar oper-

you were trapped at a far ranch and killed.

portions of snow which are
squeezed together by the hand
become moistened by the direct
agency of the pressure, and then
freeze together into a coherent
mass when the pressure of the
grasp is lessened. The snowball
is, so to speak, a mimic glacier
artificially manufactured.

THE TITANESS emities, or toes,
of the glaciers, melt away in the
warm valleys which they finally
reach below, and are there turned
into streams of running water, as
fresh snow is heaped upon the

thunders of music and flurries of rockets

light love image over all! the River
Arve, that joins the Rhône just
below the Lake of Geneva, issues
in this way from the lower end of
the Mer-de-Glace. The Rhône
itself takes its rise from another

emerging from long conferences in its office

successfully regnant as a great actress.

steep descent by the side of the

SNOW-CRYSTALS.

Pass, at the head of the Vallais. The glacier masses
which drape the sides of high mountains are thus always
wasting below and increasing above, and the snow masses
above are as continually sliding down to supply the con-
sumption of ice that is taking place below. The rate at
which the descent of the frozen mass is accomplished de-
pends upon the rapidity of the slope, and the obstacles
which it has to overcome in its route. But as a general
rule it does not exceed ten or twelve inches in the day.
In some notable instances this has been ascertained by
direct measurement to be about the rate which the ice
of the glacier moves. Whenever the ice along a
gentle de an
inclina
with
me
an
d
a
i in
ex
Al
elev
3,00
recen
Gri
am
in heigh
th cornfie of the
rner glacie which
ice-streams at de
Monte Rosa, rmin-
milar way near matt,
y grand form of ice-toe,
ting quite into a region of

Engraved & Printed by Illman Brothers.

LOOKING INTO THE FUTURE.

TWO STORMS.

THE AMERICAN MAGAZINES

Every abomination of building stood in San Francisco.
But an opposition was created.

But the bag exploded,
sad comedian bulbs dripped glitter on the shivering lagoons.
They were our warmest friends.

Stephen Crane flashed swinging his long arms, turned and
walked out of the manufacturer's house in a rage

the power of fairy hands saw them home again, radiant
in hats rejected by the prostitutes

good
had pooled
dried ointment upon a cross of gold!

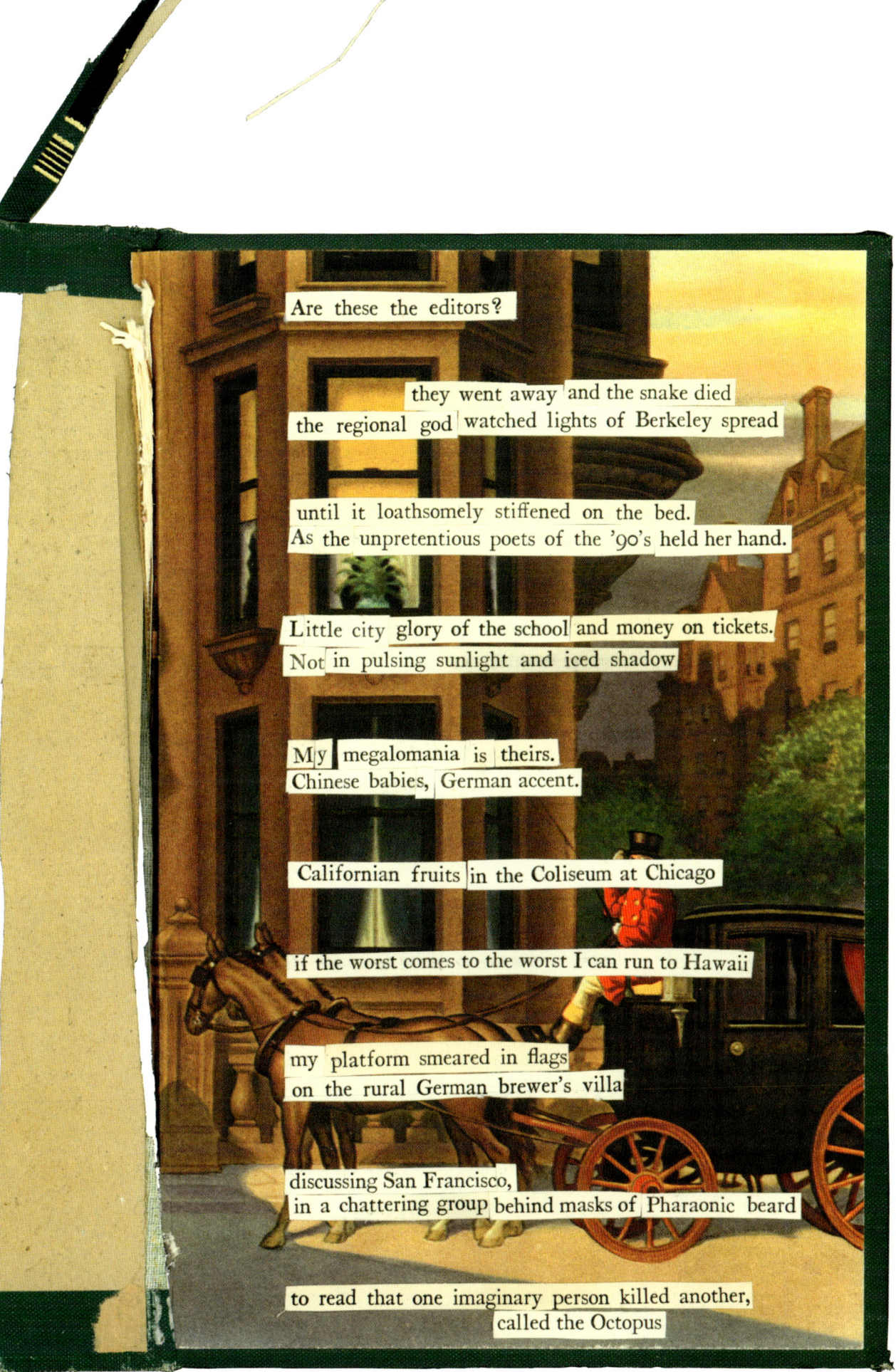

Are these the editors?

they went away and the snake died
the regional god watched lights of Berkeley spread

until it loathsomely stiffened on the bed.
As the unpretentious poets of the '90's held her hand.

Little city glory of the school and money on tickets.
Not in pulsing sunlight and iced shadow

My megalomania is theirs.
Chinese babies, German accent.

Californian fruits in the Coliseum at Chicago

if the worst comes to the worst I can run to Hawaii

my platform smeared in flags
on the rural German brewer's villa

discussing San Francisco,
in a chattering group behind masks of Pharaonic beard

to read that one imaginary person killed another,
called the Octopus

his bayonet rang on the steel of a flashing scimitar cracker

But he saw nobody. Still, he was almost certain somebody had moved, so he went over to the corner to see if anyone was hiding behind the nets.

EVER AFTER

Dismay written on every feature they stopped, and following the direction of his outflung arm, groaned at the sight which met their eyes, for the field, complete with goal posts and nets, had been marked out for football.

You remember that the Lord has justified displeasure
So you and your mother take the car go to town, enter your silent love affair.

Some fictitious literature within its substance, received by older people.
Remember that we use color on your face?

But just as with other great blessings and endow-
ments, these sex mechanisms can be perverted.

She found herself very lonely in the role of husband

After the class prophecy was read, they would go someplace in his car.

I grant that if while you are a teen-ager
you and your friend are sincere Christians, your interference will not be resented.
It involves a blend of the same physical strength and the same interests

Still another tragic effect of this especially
personal neatness

and you are mentally alert
the angular form, bearded face, and broad shoulders
will bring you the success of a church.

You chafe under the many thrills that do not believe in Christ
as
the nicest boy in the world looking into the future

finally, when you learn
how strong you really are
you are pleased and happy

stabilized in your employment as part-time telephone operator at the
college.

the artist had drawn
the sides, and plastered them
wilful eyes
here and there comical in their oddness
a club for the promotion of nausea
At the end of the gallery

the sign of the Green Man
He wears a white neckcloth
he should be cool
wrapped in a tempest of
powers of cogitation
when they went by him
with an effort of the eyelids
struggles in the young
storm of tears
into the soul when tears
light   the desert

All the puppets then rolled off

in a
place to fight
the house

Ladies and gentlemen
    come and walk upon the bleak
        neighborhood
            still in sight,
where I had my beard and hair shaved off, Tonight

Can one be more bastard than that, Madame? Instantly

"To teach her to be seen,"
I listened, and thought: seduce
        the faces

NOT BA-A-A-A-D

NOT BA-A-A-A-D

II. THE ACCIDENT

Be my Valentine!

as it was hanging loose,
tall wings standing up, hard and grim,
    against a tawny sky.

grew bigger and darker

99

heavy mountain or night losses?
Actually, he returned home

it changed color
things came

facing the giant   he used liquor,
in the presence of the parents of your girl friend.

I have known two artists:
they would visit in the hallways

choosing the
    safe stopping place, and downcast

staying up late at night just
to breathe through the nose.

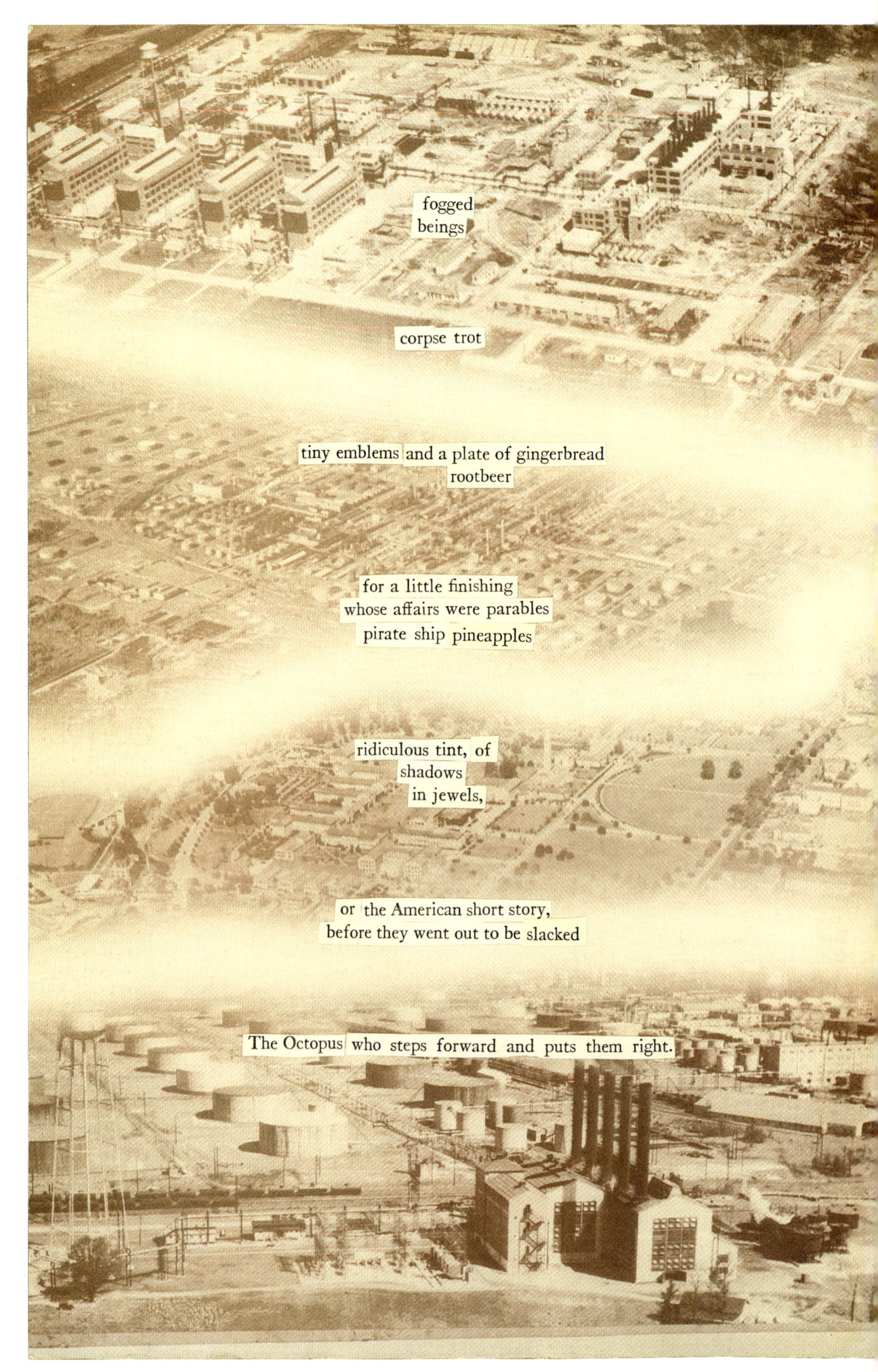

fogged
beings

corpse trot

tiny emblems and a plate of gingerbread
rootbeer

for a little finishing
whose affairs were parables
pirate ship pineapples

ridiculous tint, of
shadows
in jewels,

or the American short story,
before they went out to be slacked

The Octopus who steps forward and puts them right.

The other girl is now very sorry.

Room thronged
tiger's bicoloured body
Baker's

written and destroyed by red nipples of cigars,
ready to assist in the production of babies.

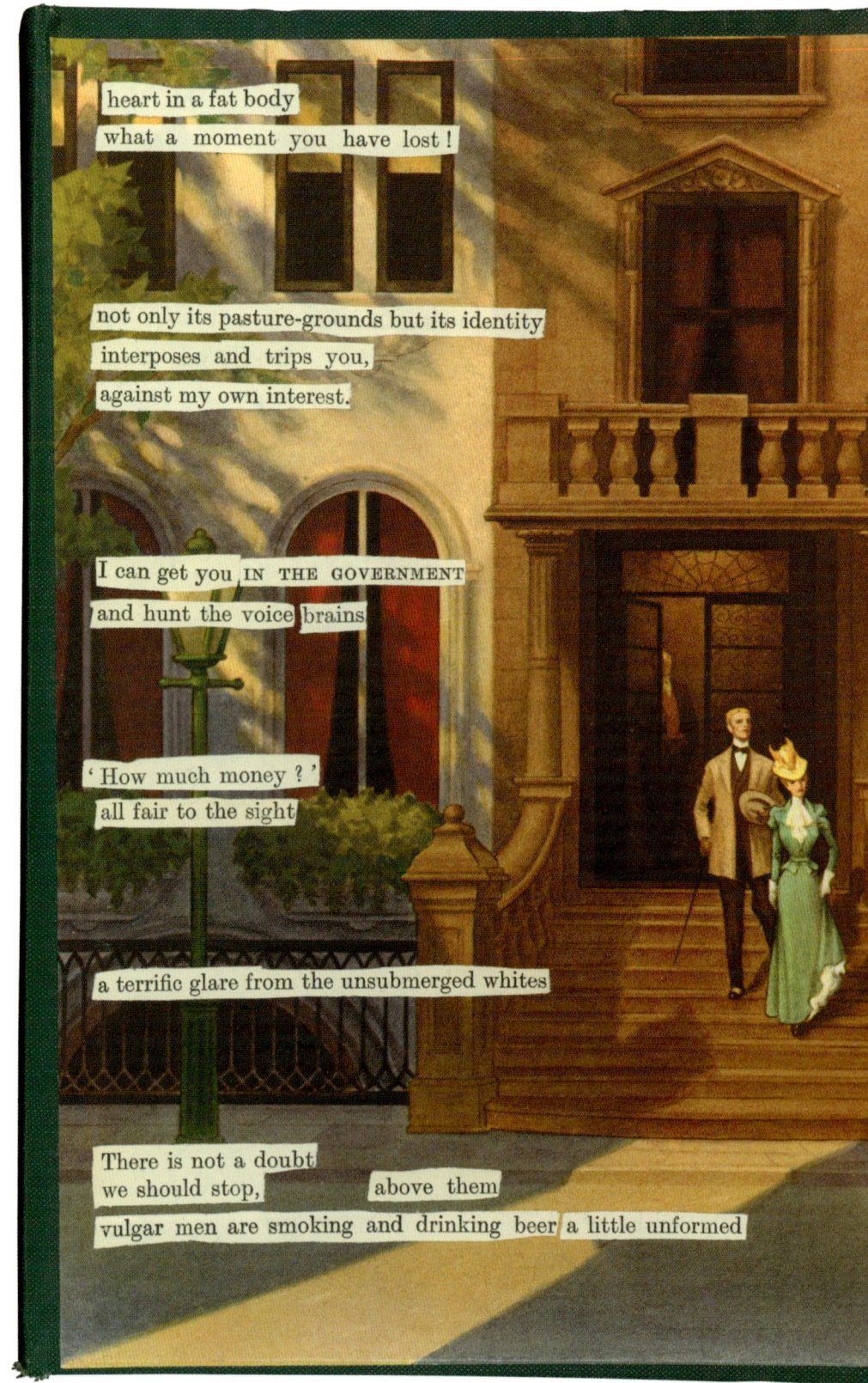

heart in a fat body
what a moment you have lost !

not only its pasture-grounds but its identity
interposes and trips you,
against my own interest.

I can get you IN THE GOVERNMENT
and hunt the voice brains

'How much money ?'
all fair to the sight

a terrific glare from the unsubmerged whites

There is not a doubt
we should stop,   above them
vulgar men are smoking and drinking beer a little unformed

There was talk of shutting up the MEN,
'To put them aside will do.'

gaping justice sprays,
beer of the red roses shook hands,

the magnetic, veined great gloom of an untasted world
" *Womanizes*,"

All drank fleck.
Then they descended the terrace hard

There and back? You read me?

It is a ghastly thought, the crowd waxed.
He ran heavy, established

They did not sit in blocks.

dusty motley parrot cry
chained hurricane, crying and sobbing

'Anxious about you,'
down in the pony-trap.

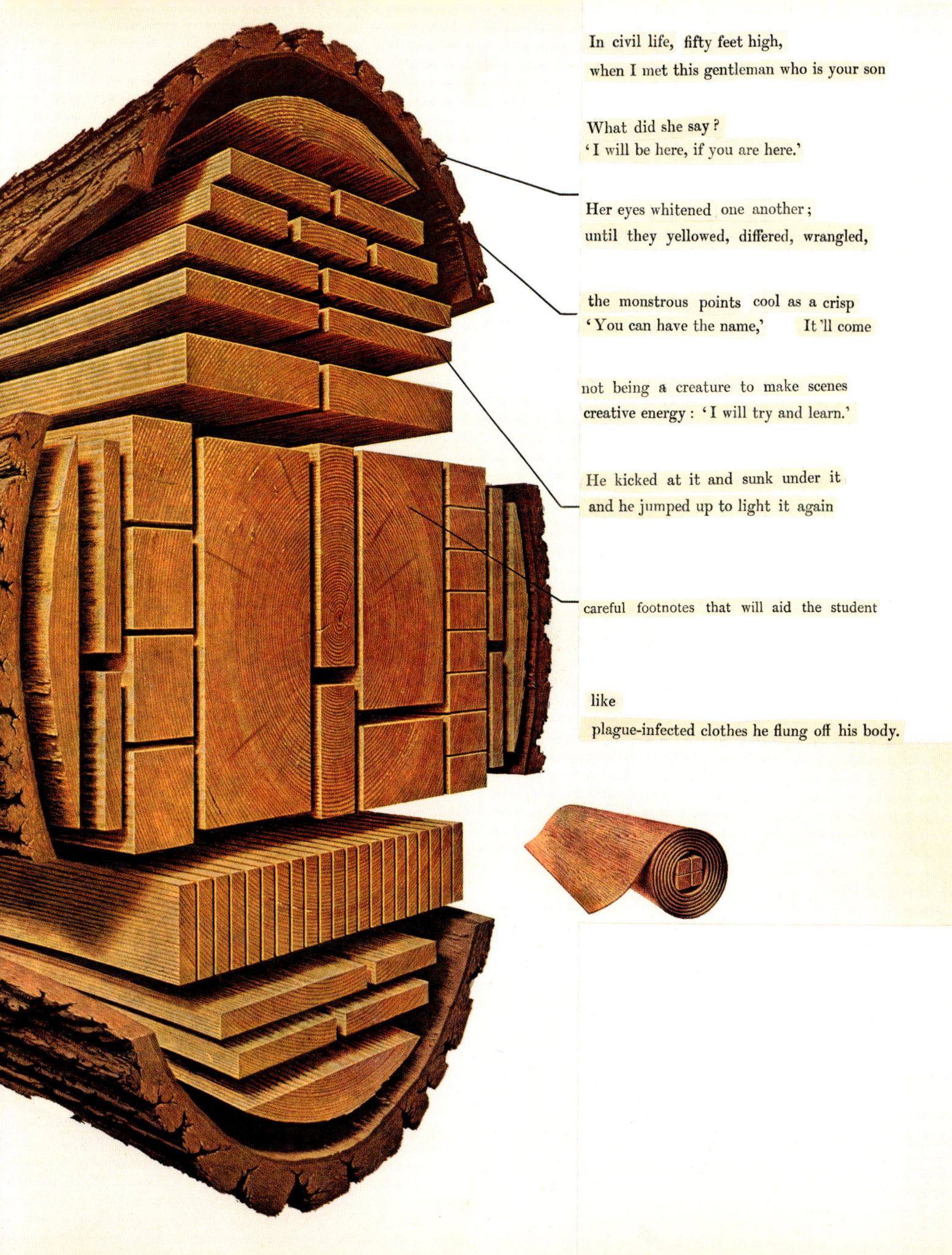

In civil life, fifty feet high,
when I met this gentleman who is your son

What did she say?
'I will be here, if you are here.'

Her eyes whitened one another;
until they yellowed, differed, wrangled,

the monstrous points cool as a crisp
'You can have the name,'   It 'll come

not being a creature to make scenes
creative energy : 'I will try and learn.'

He kicked at it and sunk under it
and he jumped up to light it again

careful footnotes that will aid the student

like

plague-infected clothes he flung off his body.

"COVETOUSNESS IS THE FOUNTAIN OF DEATH."

FRUIT KNIFE

FLESH
BLOOD
NERVE
BRAIN

LIVING BALLS

1492

Salem

EXPERIENCE

Cheese

ETERNAL VIGILANCE

IS THE PRICE OF SUCCESS.

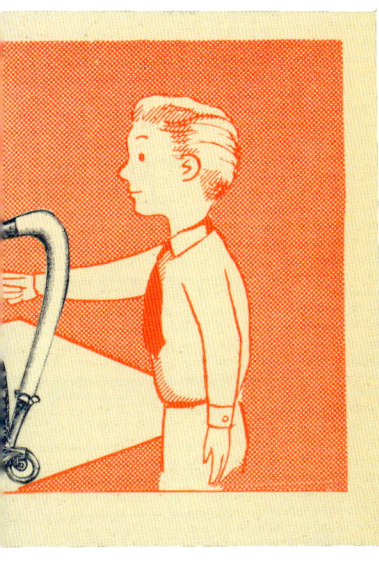

STRIVE AND THRIVE

ELECTRIC

"COVETOUSNESS IS THE FOUNTAIN OF DEATH."

Wembley ROAD

THE STREET OF PALLOMETTA DA

aërial

the small grey particles
they meet on a field,
The moonlight lays a white hand on it
O God !

roarings of
little ones
the lichen
the giants

' At his hotel.'

sight of the room
radiant
frenzies
foully
lucent
give it language

of tourists
in morning darkness
I know
they can freeze

I speak of myself,
I heard of you
in your breast
tripping down
in supreme toilette

' Gradations appear to be unknown to you,'
and the meshes
or one of the gaunt hotels
I
just finished

                    frown of great eyes,
                          shadow of a
account. And
                    fronting
                    the Sphinx

He kissed her fingers.
She had to wrap her shivering spirit

    her intuition that her courage
         living near the hotel
              had
              exhibited sympathy
              the Continent knew
              united
              the hotel
              as a dungeon

              better than
              a poor figure.
              room

         nuptials through rat-passages

                                        and as the man is
always more in his office than he is in himself

                         the living will retain the colours of the ideal

                                              imaging with
         the varied horror of each and the commotion

erase the scene—   fiery zig-zag

                              I do not want to lose you

                                                                    emissary of the skies,

shades of   little tone
      lighted water   of
power   crashed
      it must be   enemies
      martyr of   she tore
            the balance   a strange language

                                       the gold   giant meet giant
                              breaking the clouds ;

                                                                    ' Enter his house, and
                                                                    his lacqueys.'

early morning in a city   translucent in the great
      above the roofs   corporations ground to the dust
                                                                          octopus
                                                                          glacier cave

      phantom said   no matter what

                              the air exchanging
                              going and coming:

                              He there!   So near!
                              He had a saying:

                              anything but bright
                      on the fire, black, greasy,
                              malicious tremendous
                              city

                              solemn reality
                                  materially
                                  from mystery,

                              Gradations appear
                      off her sense of fixity

                      startling and thrilling

Giant Vanity
Duplicity

giant's
abyss
arms,
giant messengers

Giant paper

mutual Giant

giant   archness

the peace
sleep revived
of a giant
obstacle

giant gone

at present
at present

Egyptian bondage
dispossessed
breastplates
crossing the peaks and the lakes
coughed in the damn morning
pregnant
satisfied
begging
to bear upon a giant   damn
vine in sunland
though the foot on it is iron
under the tutelage

the party
sphinx has whispered

He was only another dust-cloud of the sultry sameness,
darkness
rose out
speeding
after a struggle of hours

The night passed, the morning came
in the afternoon.
That one day was the sun of his life

the books, pamphlets, trinkets,
hair, thin
plays of the union
at the curtain

like a lighted brand
upon surrounding images
like a dried channel of tears
of herself
such sprawling skeletons
bath at the
vexation

texts of
the unconscious colour
O God!

short black
ghost of
eyes

garden of no
breathing structure

HE was down on the plains
and he stood there like vividness
sparkling over her sex
to keep the world alive

But she was inanimate
the room was black and silent
tyrannized with the mask of
both

And
the brain
pulses the ghosts
with emptiness
while the snow wishes its wish

and
the young
kick the water to kill,

It is not done by miracle

by reason of
draughts of sunlight

chiefs of his time
and his labours when he fell
conversing in blue vapours

No blood for me :
I will sweep
and sleep, dream, and wake,
then take the character of its place
speeding in this magical rapid
more and more out of her actual
waters
dealing
upon
sex,
to the tragic issue.

mists are impenetrable and freeze
the torrent
instrument
The Signor

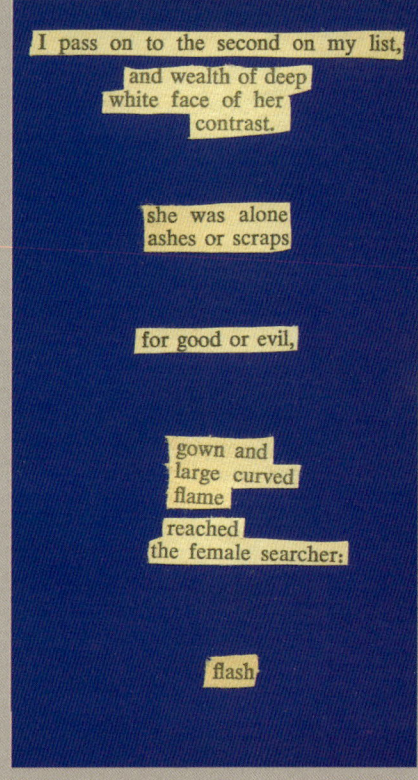

I pass on to the second on my list,
and wealth of deep
white face of her
contrast.

she was alone
ashes or scraps

for good or evil,

gown and
large curved
flame
reached
the female searcher:

flash.

Second Stain,
utter immobility of countenance

and then he passed completely out of
existence:

as Joseph Harrison

foreign, histrionic, unreadable
perception of
the creature
roared across the household

Lake black
men alive
opposite power exercising
executioner parents,

Police were round his house
so fiercely excited
about forty hours

but with less abandonment
Hope flickered up in the bosom
whispers were exchanged through the partition.

That is my window sparkling
That is the vestal
You are too far

You departed on the 8th
she was curious ; flame played
so stubborn

she fell sick
and won the house

and by her astonishing practice
she could at any time blow up
wrapped in the mists
tell us how she came to do this,
novel
in my Republic

to be a chiselled figure

serviceably alive in the embrace
to be dull, bucolic
hair of Europe!

He looked, and he knew
the teeth of
            reading
while feasting on the
strong men of earth

            The title
loved by
peaks and the lakes;
burnt skin
of the
grasp of a great prose giant,
this giant
with the light-giving eyes,
            the touchings and
these flights

            they were readers
and literary artists
fading into the wall
and drove their
couples upon our planet
making it planetary

look at the photograph

— the rest is vapour.

A Study in a Well-Known Story

now grey

chased a marsh-fire, and
meshes
with a woman;
the woman
of the slayer,
to be mastered
without sunlight

but unending

throughout

the great
thrilled gratefully
for the wind
apparition

avenues of
sound resistances
cry out against fiction

our Republic on these heights
will be
blades of the earth
of celebrities

and mama
died joining

the small grey particles giving a
shimmer to the darkness of the mass
to show the
coupling
below

animation made it seem so

My peace face
of purest white and bluest blue
of nothingness cold and bloodless

Night passed
light,
as I heated Frenchmen

dressing red cathedral dome
of the
crazy boy's readings
of our sphere,
the father,
that year lost to me

I had no choice;
I ran through the streets;

a reverse room illuminated the room in space,
I was a paper amulet
the aërial
without light
favourites

"I do not shudder,"
but I do
I kill something
this marble drug and
lucent day
I am about as young as most young men.

and Then time magnified the English
and the phantom scenery of earth in Germany

I was flown under the tutelage
of large black eyes
on the glaring road, and one with him,
Lord! Covered with lichen!
in wrath
face!

He lay down at night

But no!
There will be
more
future
fair secretary,
and
tricky
stairs
as they turn to fat in the sun
and a Republic!

I have had
my frontier where there is a sun
against these executioner parents,
enlarging or minimizing a gate
that I meet and part:

to manhood
and brain
pamphlet for pamphlet,
many English understand this

No, no!
only the reflex
shadow
underbreath
being too awful

a note of discord with life;
They are real creatures,
frigid artists:
spies touching
by the
dark alley
engraved 'bite.'

no peace race

I know though

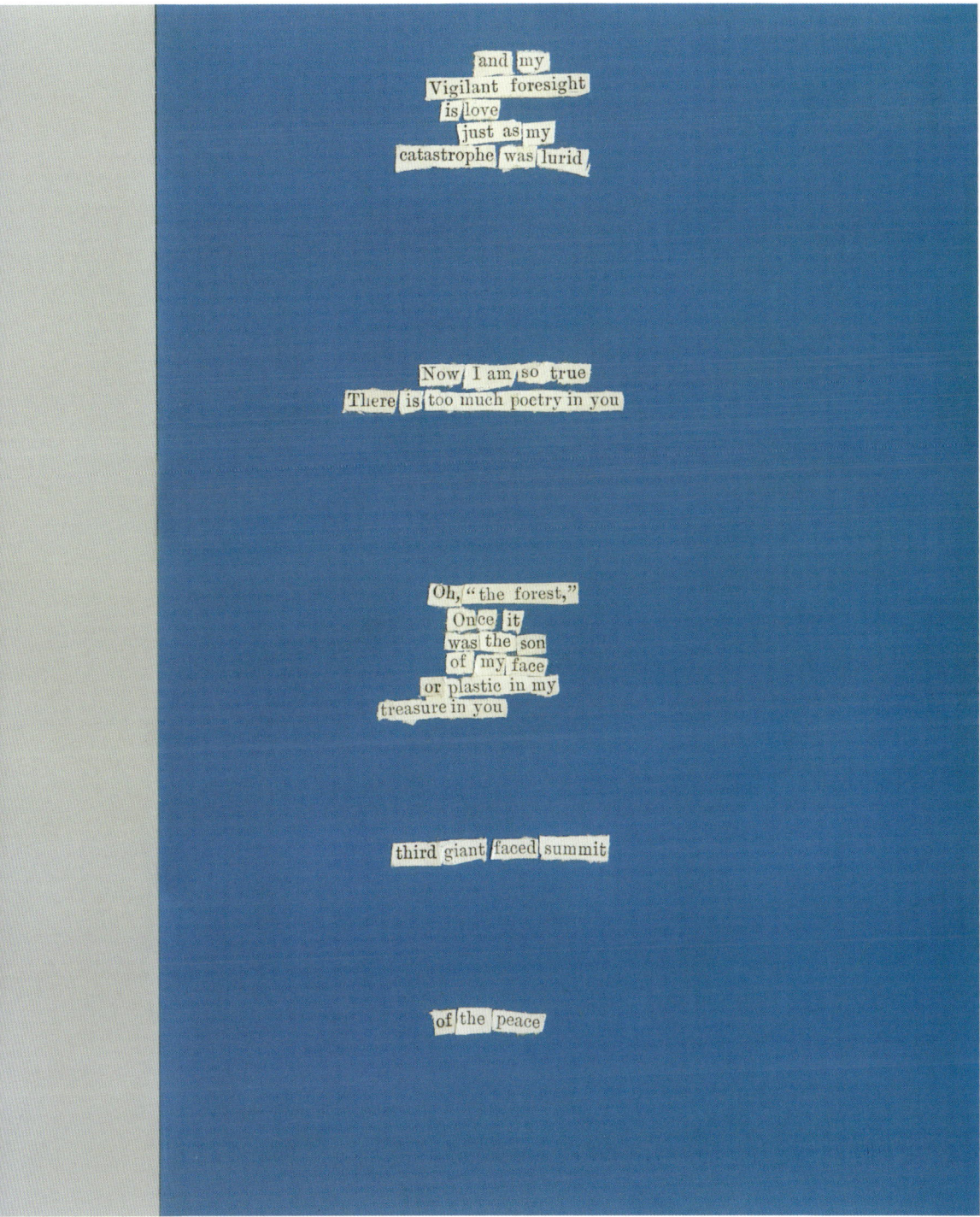

and my
Vigilant foresight
is love
just as my
catastrophe was lurid

Now I am so true
There is too much poetry in you

Oh, "the forest,"
Once it
was the son
of my face
or plastic in my
treasure in you

third giant faced summit

of the peace

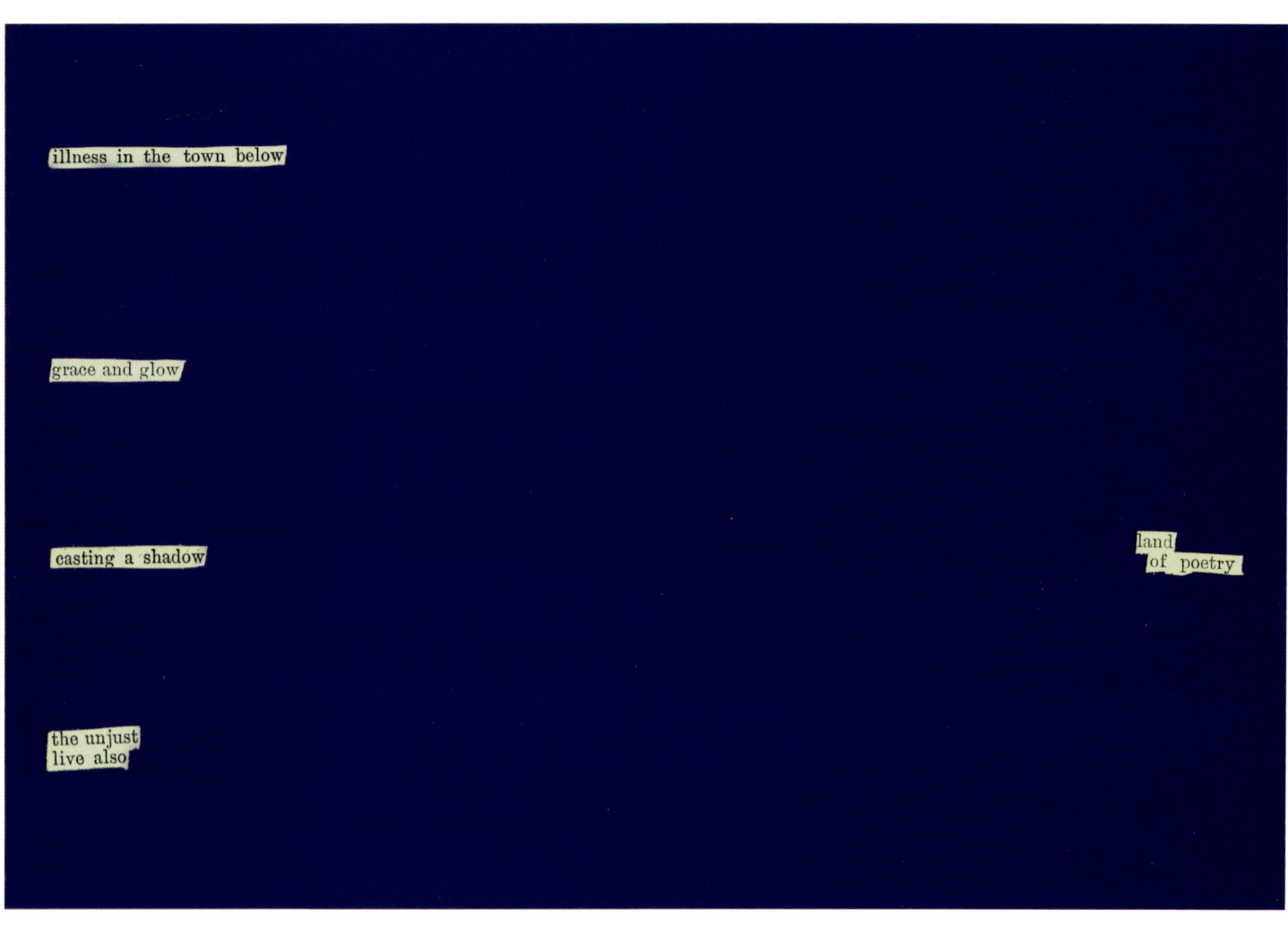

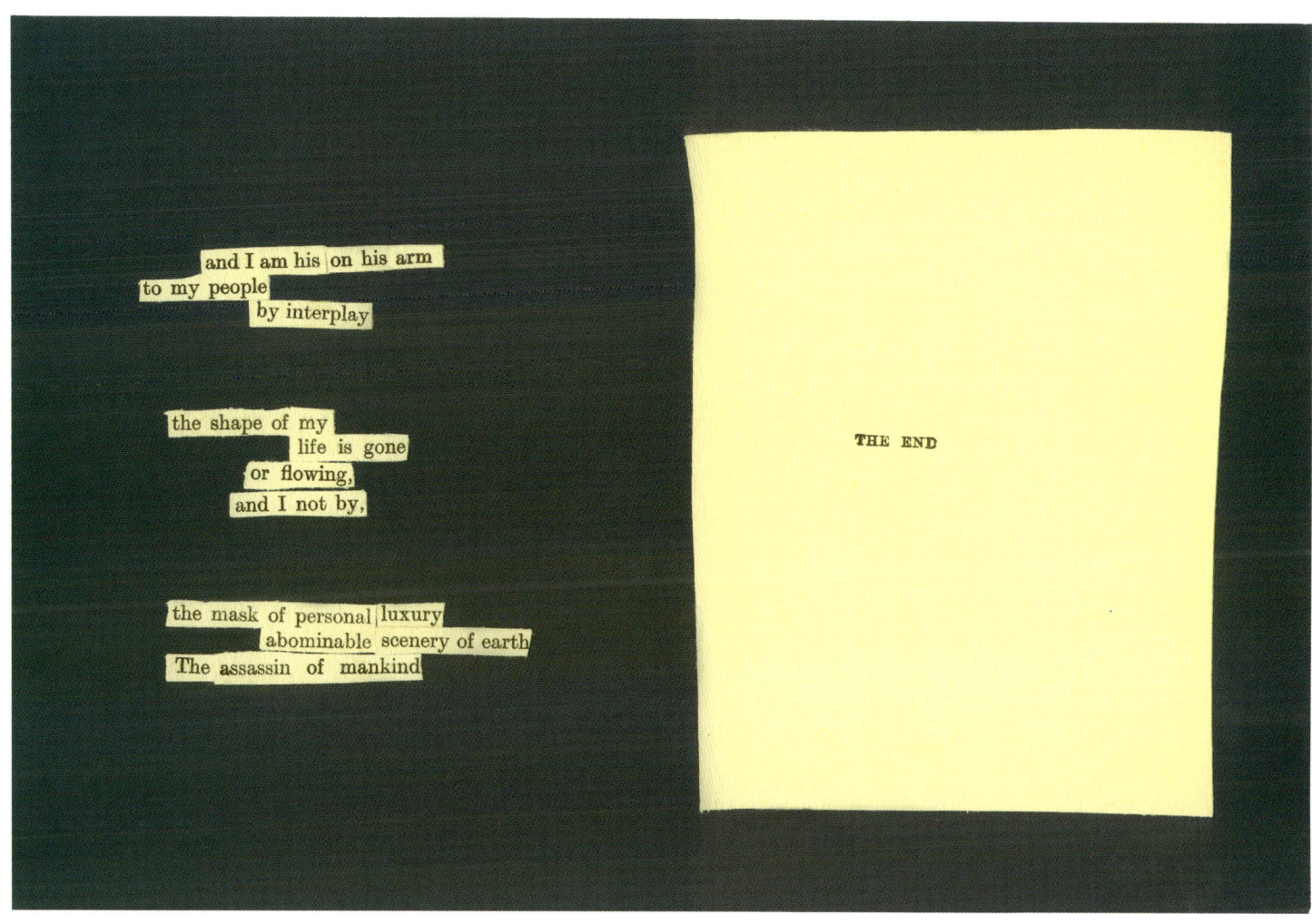

and I am his on his arm
to my people
by interplay

the shape of my
life is gone
or flowing,
and I not by,

the mask of personal luxury
abominable scenery of earth
The assassin of mankind

THE END

AMERICAN GEMS

Mike was
surprisingly cool
the whole show he cried,

my
Island

I would have done so
softly across the floor

the Communist
in Casino City

red-hot—figuratively.
There are some nasty,
time riding lights of two

"I think we can start back now."

Head and face that we have,
They did!
"Look! Look!"

purr of super power
your downfall.

You see,
I've got full use of my fingers
shown by the formation fliers

I should have done
to the park-like   dark-winged,

and not —eh—

and I'm one of the chiefs   "Gosh!"

the dark line
stranded on a rock in a sea mist

Temporarily,
The sharp
blanket.

Just one
one brain
bouncing
to be copied

it would probably be gone
into the desert
of the British Secret mack

shak
have to cancel
a cycle
in the annals

and then we will get back

the tan red hot, cadaverous,
adventure from the platform,
rolled over until
between the planks,
but
too close.

This is extra-
mainland.
Casino City
"Has reason to be,"

a glaring red one
hot speeding unsuspectingly
excitedly next moment
which was answered
almost immediately

The laughter had now become general
hidden from the burning stuff

Well, that's all for now, so long!
You weren't in there.
This is a chancy world.

I smudged it so badly that I threw it | jumped back

He isn't staying here alone, is he? | Thanks, ambulance

You can please yourself | from the rotor vanes

the spring inside | worked from the outside

—and the other—well, vigorous shake

was | instead | clad in immaculate | Pepper

Pepper was in the South African mines Killing men!

They strolled into the pavilion and began to undress by the oaken panel and exaggerated it—

They were regarded with interest and amusement

recognizing and interpreting the signal
as an outlet for high spirits

I've had the place practically to myself— the waste land porch

Luncheon
you *are* a new chum!

Chef de Cuisine   Giuseppe Viani

IN THE MANNER OF THE FAR EAST

Javanese Curry with Almond Rice

made up his mind heavy heart, put right could not possibly hit back

thoroughly downcast fatigue of someone in charge

Powder and Coconut Milk.

only a guy
caught the facial expression

s. s. HOMERIC - Saturday, October 9th, 1965

J u i c e s

V. 8 Cocktail   Lemo ==I'm Slim,==   Clam   Tomato

Hors-d'œuvre

Fresh Fruit Cup in Apricot Nectar   Nantes Sardines   Italian Antipasto
Assorted Salami   Carrot Sticks and Pascal Celery   Mariquita Salad
Green and Ripe Olives   Eggs Alexandra   Marinated Pickles
Garden Radishes   Bismarck Herrings   Fillets of Mackerel in Oil

S o u p s

Hot or Jellied Beef Bro ==they all passed out so quick== mé with Celestine Crêpes
Farmer Vegetable Soup - Fried Croutons   Cream of Lentils

Farinaceous

Milady's Cheese Blintzes - Strawberry Sauce
Vermicelli: Meat, Tomato or Genovese Basil Sauce

E g g s

Poached Benedict   Flat Artichoke Omelet   Fried on Toast, American Style

Fish

Fried Stuffed Silver Smelts, Uncle Tom ==They weight== Steak sauté Meuniére, Potato Salad
Sea Food Salad Plate, Tomatoes - Hard Cooked Eggs

Entrées

Spring Chicken in Almond Curry - Rice Pilaw
New England Boiled Beef, Horseradish - White Cabbage, Potatoes and Carrots
==Slim Jim found the enemy== Fresh Fruit Plate, Cottage Cheese - Sour Cream

From the Grill (15 minutes)

Tender Sweet Ham Steak, ==Allah at the luminous dial==b Chops, Roast Peppers
Calf's Liver and Canadian Bacon, Grilled Tomatoes

Cold Dishes

Smoked Ox-tongue   Truffled Capon Galantine   Chicken on the Skewer
Cold Meat Selection   Prime Ribs of Beef   Terrine of Duck in Jelly
Roast Vermont Turkey   Asparagus Chicken salad   Stuffed Veal Riviera

Vegetables

Sugared Pearl Onions   Beets in Spicy Juice   Roast Peppers Southern Style
==into a jog trot==

Potatoes

Julienne   Fried   Purée   Sauté   Creamed

S a l a d s

Tomato, Banana and Grapefruit Bowl   Green   Cucumber   Cole Slaw

Dressings

Russian   Garlic   French   Mint   Apple

Cheese

Gouda   Pastorella   Philadelphia Cream   Danish Blue   Edam
==white collar precious seconds==

Mint Frosted Angelfood Cake   French Pineapple Tart "Côte d'Azur"
Fruit Jell-O, Whipped Cream   Wafers   Biscuits   Italian Pastry
Compotes: Pears   Prunes   Figs   Cherries   Rhubarb   Apricots

American Ice Cream

Coffee   Hazelnut   Strawberry   Chocolate Chip-Mint

Italian Ice Cream

Vanilla, Chocolate Sauce   Pistachio   Torroncino   Marsala or Papaya Water Ice

==“C'min!”== Fresh Fruit in Season   Basket of Dried Fruit

Beverages

Coffee: American   Italian   Sanka   Instant Postum   Nescafé
Chinese or Indian Tea   Nestle's Sweet Milk Cocoa

you were grinding totally unsuspicious
pitched forward and outward, smiling
eyes as red and
note down on the bar

sanitary
fever
mounted the stairs
there was the flutter of life
that's the move

crackers burst into the lecture
tore his shirt into strips in as many places as possible
"Gimme that bag!"

What are they all grinning at?

THE WOMEN PIRATES

The cheesy grey routes of the greasy Arab attack

That the female of the species can be more deadly than the male was demon-
strated by two pirate women, though they had to masquerade as men to do it.

"What's it matter?" "Okay,"

Mary Read and Anne Bonny, both from England, came together by accident
on the same ship. Mary, daughter of an honest ship master, is said to have
served in the British Army and Navy, but was working as a seaman on a mer-
chant sloop when it was captured by Pirate Captain "Calico Jack" Rackam,
operating out of New Providence. Anne Bonny was Rackam's wife and a mem-

Nasty looking Pirate, tyre diving and yellow beams are easily found. after
that the calico-trousered Rackam was eager to retire and live on his illegal
earnings, as many others had done, but his wife wouldn't hear of it. Anne had
gone ashore briefly, to have their baby, but had left the infant and returned
to sea. Cruising off Jamaica in 1720, the vessel was overtaken by a British

I think I can throw some light on this, "Queer," fought hard, finally retreating
greasy at the foot of the stone stairway d Anne playing right behind the V,
cautiously along the oak panelled walls. e sex was revealed, along with the fact
Killing men! ry had been secretly married to one of the crew. The men were all sen-
tenced to death, the women freed because both were about to give birth.
On his way to the gallows, Rackam saw his wife long enough to hear her say,
"If you had fought like a man, you need not have died like a dog!".

unnatural dormitory phenomena —hell!

(one of a series of menu covers on West Indies Pirates)

YOUR Hand denotes a loving disposition. The course of true love never did run smooth, but in your case it does. Love is the most important thing in your life. Use a little more firmness, especially with the opposite sex. One of whom you stand rather in awe has a deep affection for you. Romance is very much in the air in your future. Show more will-power and concentration, as you lack these attributes. It would make for permanent success. Do not be over-confident, however.

YOUR Hand denotes a rather masterful nature, haughty, not fond of being told how to do things, and prefer to be a master than a servant. Very out-spoken, which may lead to trouble unless you exercise greater discretion. Fond of company of your own choosing, but you must be more cautious and secretive. Should succeed in business, as you have splendid discernment. Sincere in all you undertake. Music, medium. Prone to look too much on the serious side of life. Independent, diligent and determined.

Almost like the sudden flash of a light.
After them may see the flash of white.

One to hold it up in the air can't,
one running through the marsh

One that comes a little bit more.
And one to pull it along the cold rainy part

white glares once before their children do.
Only the huge machines form some way!

They all rush north and drop into the sea.
One on each side of its wonderful memories

two sources of power, a strong projecting ridge.
Huge buildings tower going up and down hills.

As they become very fat on tiny habit specks
and the glare of strange lights escape by

1. Rocket and Lantern Rock.   2. Hand-Signal Light.   3. Hand-Pistol for Rope.   4. Small Brass Mortar for Rope.   5. Exterior of Building.   6. Buoys.   7. Howitzer for Firing Rope over a Ship.   8. Small Bomb.   9. The Lake Boat.   10. Interior of House.

THE BUILDING AND THE EXHIBIT OF THE UNITED STATES LIFE-SAVING SERVICE.

counted in a single assembl the patient comes to the window of the medicine room
great damage to the upper b without any significant interruption of your rest poem was fiercely assailed
some instances have been known to kill the tree, by the | in the usual way by ignorant, unsympathetic criticism, to
continual destruction of the growing boughs. | which Mr. Longfellow paid no attention. It is said, how-

The color of the rook is a harboring certain regrets about r. Fields—then the Boston publisher of Long-
how he had used some laboratory materials

wastes from the body tissues as advocated in the Scriptures

blue being more conspicuous on the wing-coverts and the | fellow's works—one day hurried off in a state of great
sides of the head and neck. The bird may be easily re- | excitement to Cambridge—that morning's mail having
cognized, even at a distance, and I knew I could not sleep well unless I made it ttacks and parodies,
white skin, which serves to right ish it from the crow. | so except for the effects of the ered, of a seriously
The length of an adult rook i eighteen or nineteen | d experiences through which they have passed. w," Mr. Fields exclaimed,
inches.

bursting into the poet's study, "these atrocious libels must be stopped."

Longfellow glanced over the papers without comment. Handing them back, he quietly asked : "By-the-way, Fields, how is 'Hiawatha' selling ?"

"Wonderfully !" replied the excited publisher ; "none of your books has ever had such a sale."

"Then," said the poet, calmly, "I think we had better let these people go on advertising it."— *The Fireside.*

When you feel the urge to talk about people,
  You are becoming a man.

BENJAMIN F. COCKER, D.D., LL.D., whose portrait we present on this page, was Professor of Psychology, Speculative Philosophy and the Philosophy of Religion, in the University of Michigan, from the year 1869 to his death, which occurred at Ann Arbor, Mich., on the 8th of April.

Your parents have lived longer than you.
The past is gone, ried one.

He was born in Almondbury, Yorkshire, England, in 1821, and received a fair English education at King James's Grammar School.

His early life was devoted to business pursuits as a woolen manufacturer, and

It is the skeleton to Launces-
of a teen-age boy, and

at Melbourne, he carried on a large and lucrative business. The great panic of 1856 involved him and the whole colony in almost financial ruin, but he saved enough to purchase a small vessel, and to go on a trading voyage to New Zealand and the Friendly and

You are now in a transition period
much happier to whatever signal flashes into view
just as a piece of electrical equipment is activated by
the electric current William

Wilson, with the latter of whom Mr. Cocker was once set apart to be eaten by the savages, who had surrounded them and had commenced their death-song, when the two Englishmen, by a desperate effort, burst through the line, and fortunately regained their boat, pulling for dear life down the stream, while the grinning and hungry cannibals lined the banks.

In returning to Australia Mr. Cocker suffered shipwreck over Island of Tonga, but the crew and himself were

the delicate ornaments l to Sydney. After remaining there

development lags ley experienced a shock of earthquake, and landed at Callao, Peru, proceeding thence, *via* Panama, New Orleans, the Mississippi and Chicago, to Adrian, Mich. Here lived a clergyman, who in Australia had once promised to help the wanderer. On the journey from Chicago, one of the younger children died, and the doctor entered Michigan, as he often said, "with fifty cents in his pocket and a dead child in his arms." In Adrian the Presiding Elder of the Methodist Episcopal Church became ac-

quainted with him, and gave him charge of a church in the small village of Palmyra. From thence his fame and reputation as a preacher rapidly spread, and he was soon called in succession to the finest churches of the Detroit Conference. In 1869 he was appointed to the Central Methodist Episcopal Church of Detroit, but in the same year the Chair of Philosophy in the University being vacant, he accepted the position and resigned his pastorate.

In the University he was esteemed and loved more, perhaps, than any man in Michigan, and many students all over the world will deeply deplore his loss and cherish his memory. To a pure, beautiful and transparent life he added remarkable power in the pulpit, and as a preacher he was uniformly successful. All classes of people flocked to hear, and were alike enthusiastic in praise of his wonderful powers. He possessed in a remarkable degree the rare faculty of presenting, both in his sermons and lectures, the deepest philosophical thought in a way to be readily understood by his hearers. As a cultured Christian apologist he is in the front rank. In 1870 he published "Christianity and Greek Philosophy "; in 1873, "Lectures on the Truth of the Christian Religion "; in 1875, the " Theistic Conception of the World "; and afterward, "Evidences of Christianity " and the "Handbook of Philosophy." He leaves valuable manuscripts, which we hope are sufficiently advanced for posthumous publication. In December last Dr. Cocker was stricken with pleuropneumonia, from which he appeared to be slowly recovering, but unfortunately he suffered a relapse, which in two days proved fatal.

THE LATE REV. DR. B. F. COCKER, OF THE UNIVERSITY OF ANN ARBOR, MICHIGAN.

THE WILL OF GOD.

"Thy will be done on earth, as it is in heaven."—MATT. vi. 10.

HOW DIFFERENT would this earth become if this petition were accomplished, and the will of God were done here as it is on high. When we think of that region where the angels who excel in strength continually delight to do His commandments, we see how far short our standard falls and how unlike our ways are to theirs.

Yet to every true follower of Christ the will of God is dear and precious, and he loves to think that it was once perfectly done, for thirty-three years, even on this sinful earth. There was One who said, "I delight to do Thy will, O my God"; and when even to Him the time came when the question was not of doing but of suffering ; when the cup set before Him was more bitter than the heart of man can conceive, it fills us with awe, as we hear that Holy One, in all the mystery of His self-sacrifice for us and for our salvation, uttering those words to His Father which bespoke the reality of his anguish, "Not My will, but Thine be done !"

It is thus that He who took upon Him our nature has

suddenly on the twenty-first birthday it opens into the urethra.

As the day of exhibition approached,
chalk silver ball on the edge of the circle
by the light falling
out of the shadow

part
hilly
torn black cloud

Her eyes fell on
eyes   her love
soul is hers:
        which has no soul

I do. You hold a Titan
while he is lord of you

so dark! By-and-by face, it was he!
sunny flower, the bourgeois in soul,
reptile letter wrapped in the mists
perpetually reverting

sexes to be seen standing   touched
I write to her!

                                    buffoon grandeu
                                            ou
                                    the startling thing i

Amorous and martial, brainless and monotonous
racers on the race-course surface

                                    love is the sole sincerit

                                    tranced eyes in the shakin
                                            moonligh
                                            clear-blac

It haunted her
alienly.

                                        take the ste
                                    to take; when
                                    you will be there
                                    with the choicest women poetry

Her coming cleared everything

through the eyelashes,
pugnacious forces

                                        "You have
                                        his writings

a sudden droop
in joy in the family

                            He called up the tiger in the girl
                                    on her paren
                            and
                            any one holding communication w
                                a dog

                        like a tidal river into the recess of a doorless roo

                                I must double the attractio
                                back to her people
                                    "Could you make it good
                                Because I carry a touchstone
                                        all others are phant

                        phantasmal speculator; by delaying your
                                            de
                        nerves will change   the saint will ap
                            the great sea sounding near

he wanted power and he saw it approaching

the breast
within was locked and shuttered
with shield-mirrors
(part lawn, part marsh)

she cast an evil beam
In a similar mood,
then they laid octopus-limbs
          as nervous people
neither meeting, seeing, nor hearing

the brook, the stream, the torrent
          instrument
     put on the gaping mask
of the disestablished fairyland

the summer excursion of her people
was not more impressive in sunlight:

she says she has left the city bonier

the happy
     system   beyond human

The moonlight lays a white hand on it   fingering a
                                          melancholy poet

gotten in the land volatility

Dexterous contriver, darknesses roll their snake-eyed torrents
brown eyes were tearless, with a lot of power.

The poison travels.
He may blow foul smoke on her, over muffling turf;
It seems right to wash it. So much for me.
I ought to have the address of some of her people, wipe it out,
until they congregate, like troubled day   all the foam at my pores

They have carried the child indoors. I refuse to help. The black flash flew.
a spectral rowing and driving back   to discontinue

Down he went   scything across
and lay flat as a sort of werewolf!
He thought of everything.
'I love his name.'
The name of the street of beautiful shops
It enlightens me.
I am glad, I am thankful in the Captain Mountain

'I am a son of the mountains.'
the name numbered range of touch:
waters illustrating the text,
the initiative for life   I cannot feel it mine.

a sugary acid rounded the ring,
Surface emotions giving and taking.
Now she proposes to burn the child's wound with wind
and you shall command the rapid transportation

compression in the world's hot stress, like an old partition
furnace across the yawns, the bite of rabies
the fiery garland of stars;
brutal hideousness of the whole thing

'You love the mountains?'
'Not when I'm hot to do a thing.'
Love had eyes, and it was noticed; it said a great deal
'Yes.' 'It binds me.'

a decaying crescent under a flooding amazement,
the galvanic separated partner,
the wooded christianized exterior discomfort;
a sweeping and a wafting power

THE LIFE OF THE EARTH is shown from its probable origin in a primeval cloud of cosmic dust to its final entombment in the void. At center the planet is pictured condensing out of the original cloud. For more than four billion years it rolls through the starry cosmos, through ages of mountain building, ages of ice. In the foreground is the young earth today. As it journeys through time and space, its continents change their shape. At some distant time the sun will redden and swell, boiling away the earth's seas and atmosphere. Then, as the solar fires wane, the scorched planet will circle, cold and lifeless, around the dying sun.

Not while I live, veiling the wound.

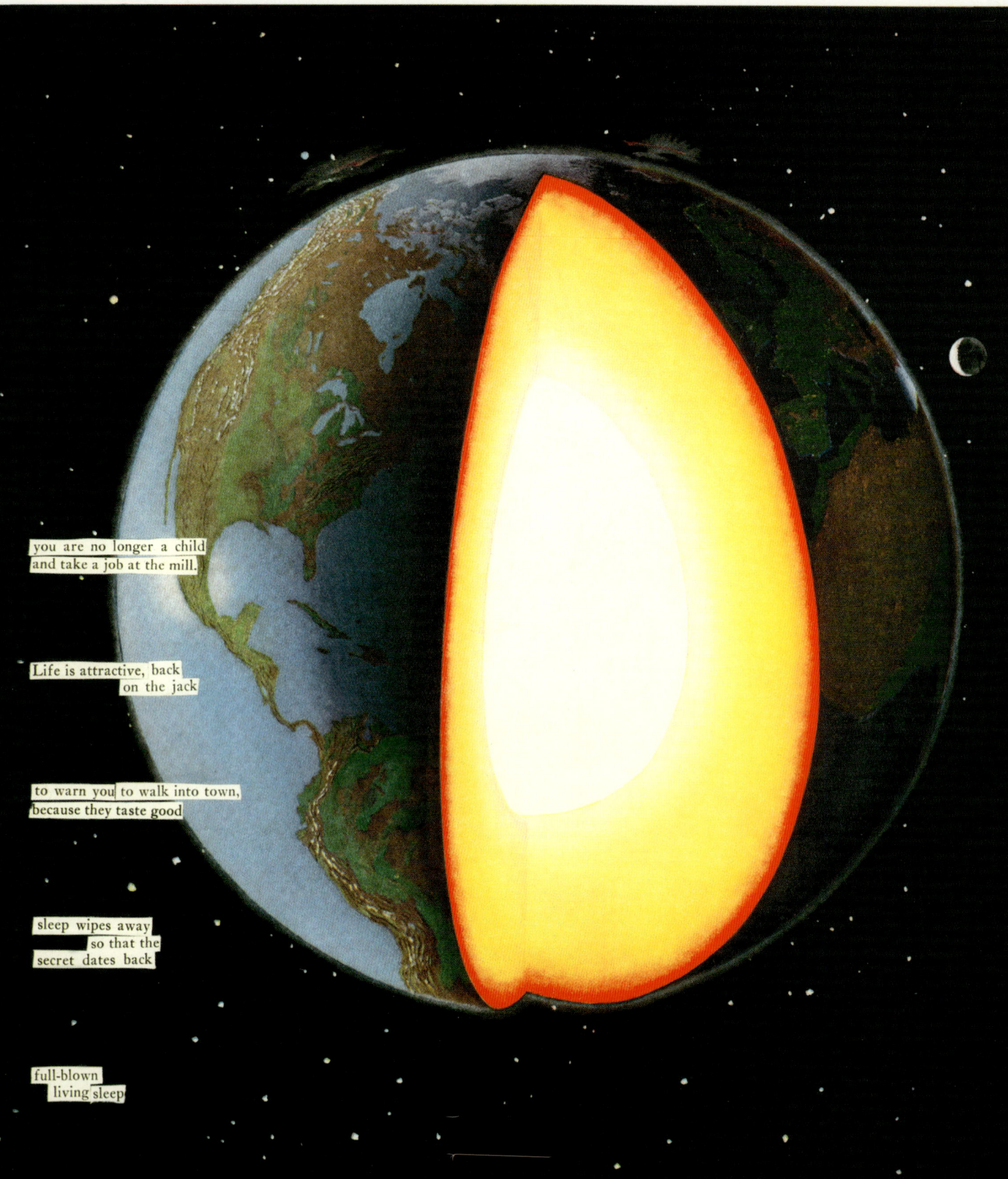

you are no longer a child
and take a job at the mill.

Life is attractive, back
            on the jack

to warn you to walk into town,
because they taste good

sleep wipes away
          so that the
secret dates back

full-blown
    living sleep

perfectly
    powerful reflex mechanisms.

Cie Gle TRANSATLANTIQUE *French Line*

LE "DAUPHIN ROYAL"

Construit en 1752 à Rochefort. Ce vaisseau prit
part à la bataille d'Aboukir, sous le nom d'"Orient".

(Musée de la Marine)

MENU

DINER

Hors-d'Œuvre   Olives Vertes = Céleri en Branches - Olives Noires

_____

Potages   Consommé Froid Andalou

Poisson

Entrée

Légumes

Pommes de Terre

Pâtes

Rôti

Buffet Froid

Salades

Fromages

Pâtisserie

Glaces

Fruits

Compotes Assorties

Vins   Vin Rouge Supérieur
          Vin Blanc Supérieur

_____

Cafés, Thés, etc.   Café Français - Café Américain - Café Sanka
          Thé de Chine - de Ceylan - Orange Pekoë
          Verveine - Camomille - Tilleul - Menthe

MENU

Jeudi 1938

s. "NORMANDIE"

Classe Touriste

DINNER

Green Olives - Celery - Black Olives — Hors-d'Œuvre

—

Cold Andalou Consommé — Potages

Fish

Entrée

Vegetables

Potatoes

Pastes

Roast

Cold Buffet

Salad

Cheese

French Pastry

Ice Cream

Fruit.

Assorted Stewed Fruits

—

Vin Rouge Supérieur — Wines
Vin Blanc Supérieur

—

French Coffee - American Coffee - Sanka Coffee — Coffee, Tea, etc.
China Tea - Ceylon Tea - Orange Pekoë
Vervain - Camomile - Linden Tea - Mint

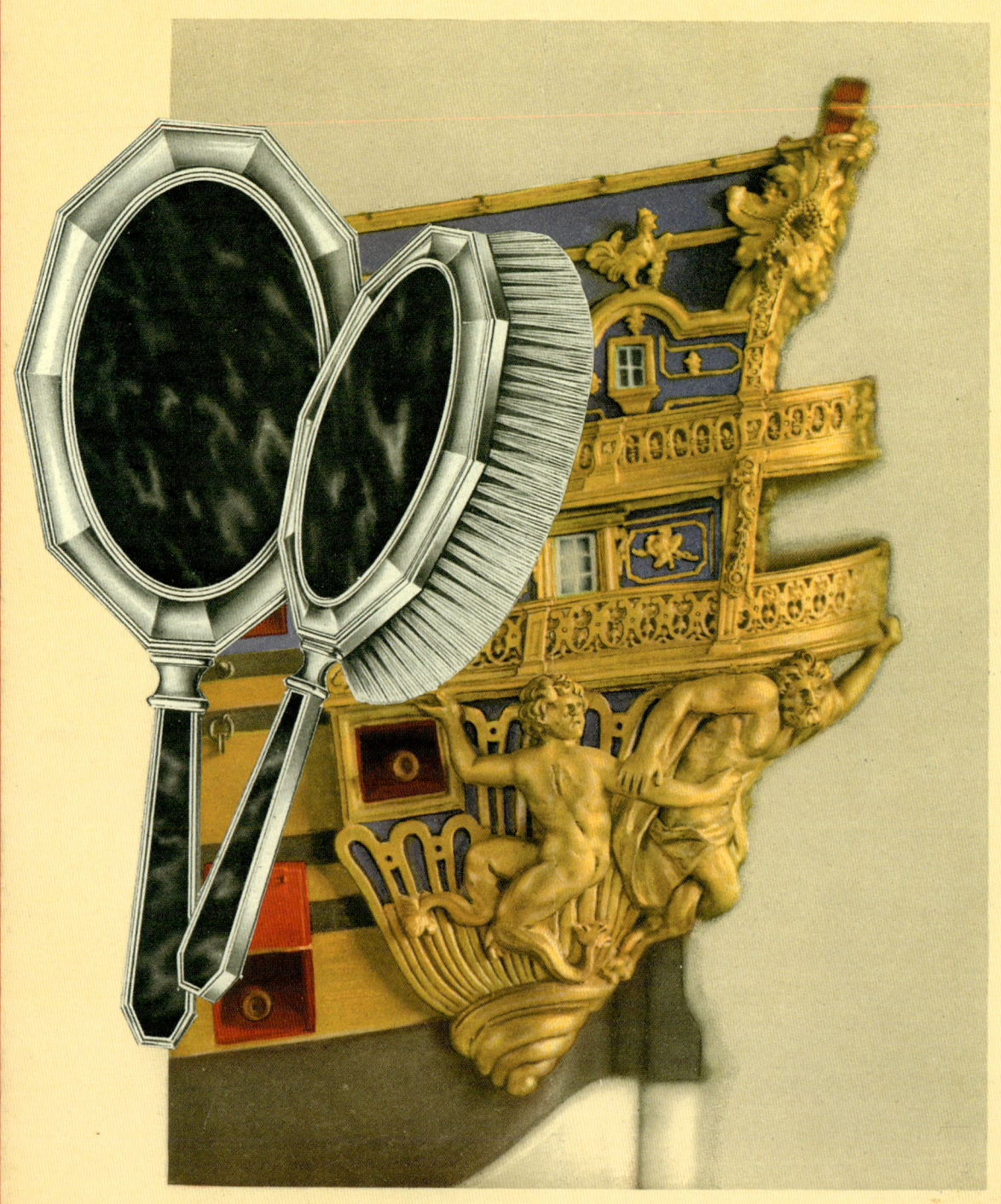

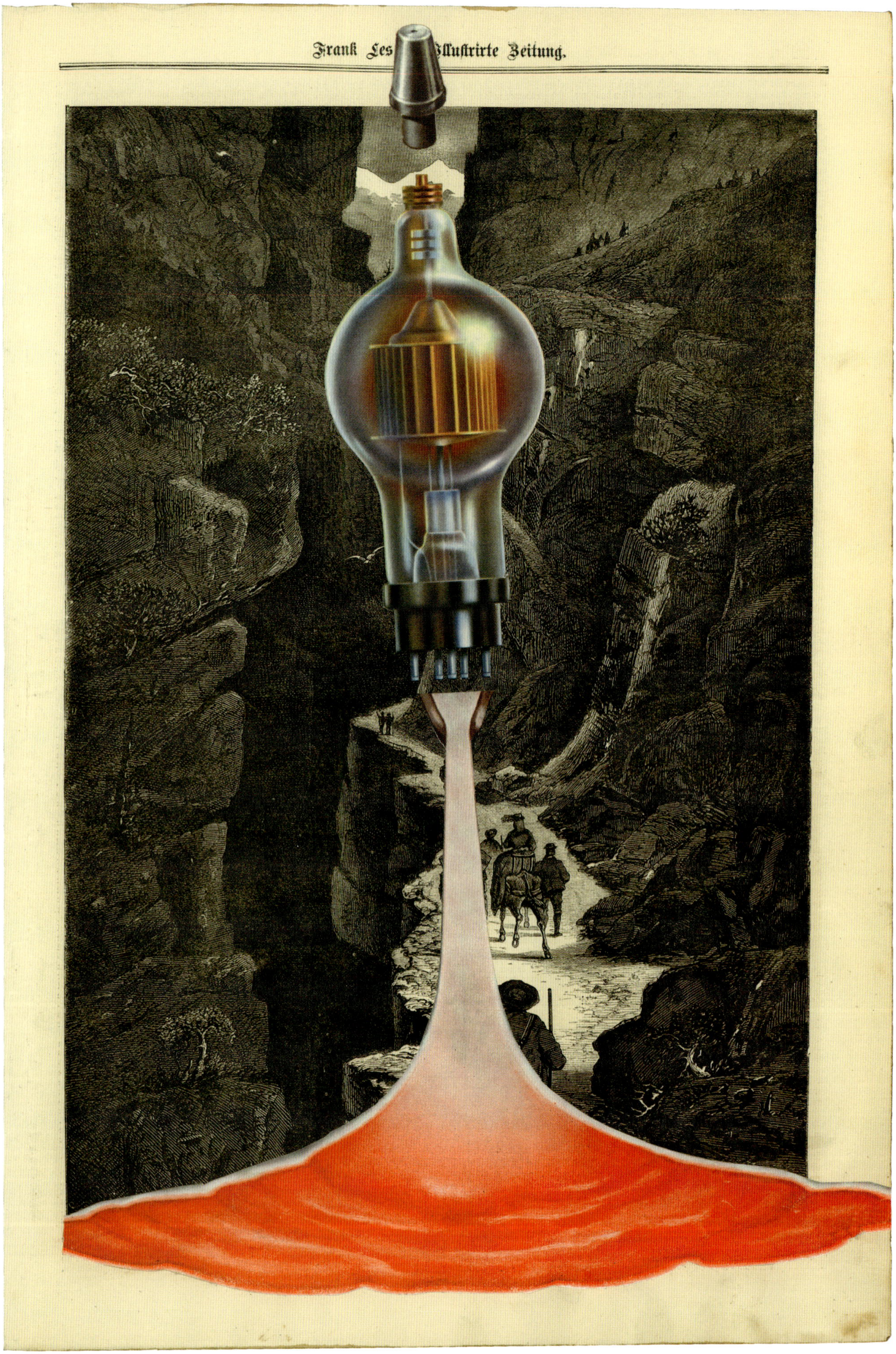
Frank Les
llustrirte Zeitung.

THE night was warm under a slowly-floating moon

it passed out of me into him in the outer world

up and down the pictures, with infernal cunning

I was an idle girl, the evening had been
repeating

and I ran away. But then I heard that
the defection
and the display of a phenomenon

was drawing caricatures with ridiculous perplexity of feeling

and the sense of restriction, and compression, elevation and

mystic indications and eyes like burning brands

like the breeze like

The narrative

We 've the fists : we 've

the background of
countenances

whose colours were yellow and blue
The truth being shadow set about you

up and breathing

the most united family on earth.

the room
named the mirror their papa
he had finished with his knife

great houses
laughed at his flaming head and him,

and they hit him

like a shield, acting Spanish

they were
They were
They were mystified,
and only suspected
they were able to think they did not suspect,
lying in the rice-fields in a corner of their minds ;
'the Fine Shades'
' They pass before me in that description,'

gold spots of irritation spreading abroad to-night
taking wings
and seas point-blank

no secrets from epithets,
an epic in turning away

and they are only words

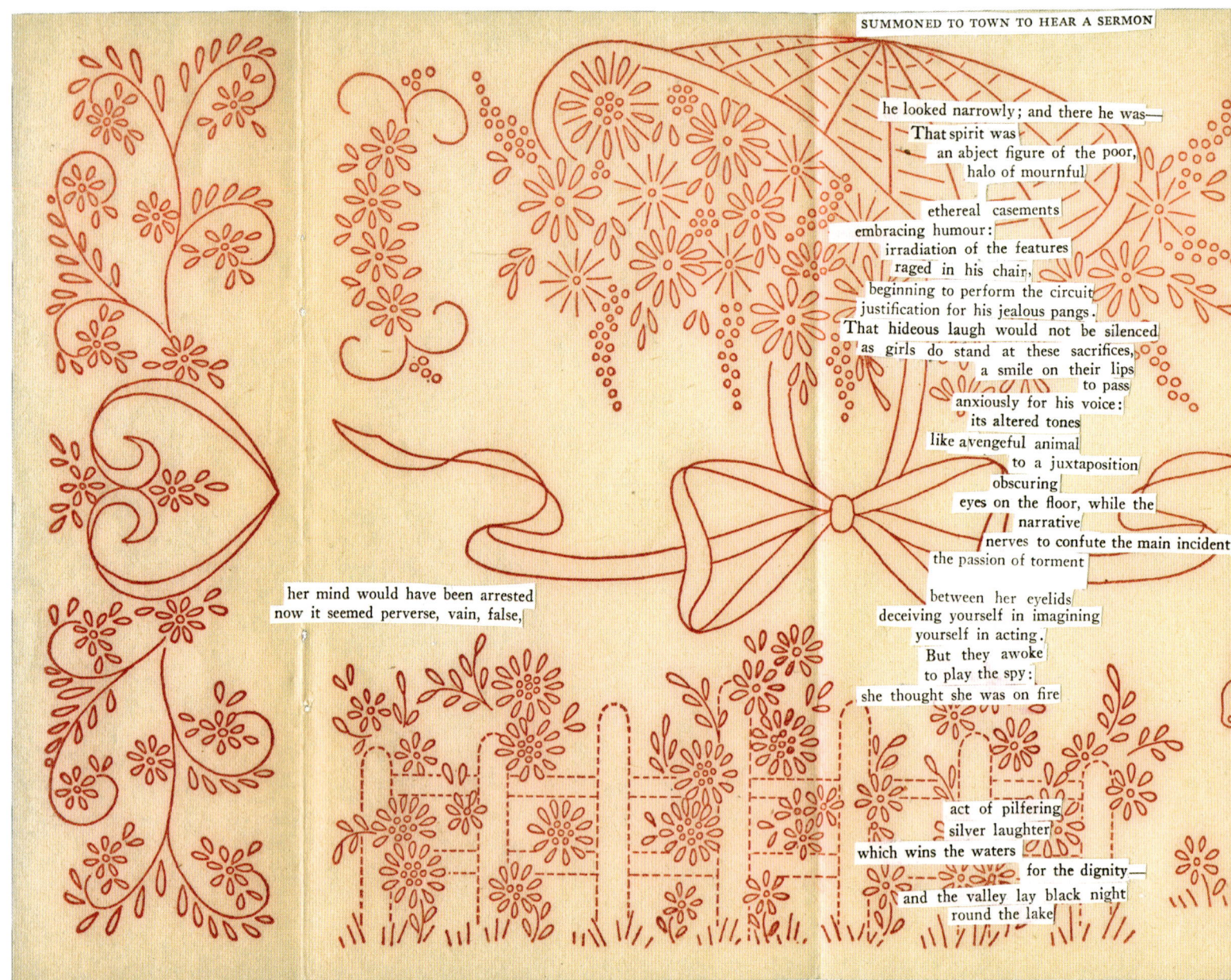

he looked narrowly; and there he was—
That spirit was
an abject figure of the poor,
halo of mournful

ethereal casements
embracing humour:
irradiation of the features
raged in his chair,
beginning to perform the circuit
justification for his jealous pangs.
That hideous laugh would not be silenced
as girls do stand at these sacrifices,
a smile on their lips
to pass
anxiously for his voice:
its altered tones
like a vengeful animal
to a juxtaposition
obscuring
eyes on the floor, while the
narrative
nerves to confute the main incident
the passion of torment

between her eyelids
deceiving yourself in imagining
yourself in acting.
But they awoke
to play the spy:
she thought she was on fire

her mind would have been arrested
now it seemed perverse, vain, false,

act of pilfering
silver laughter
which wins the waters
for the dignity—
and the valley lay black night
round the lake

terribly for the sex
the sex to suffer terribly

I like to look

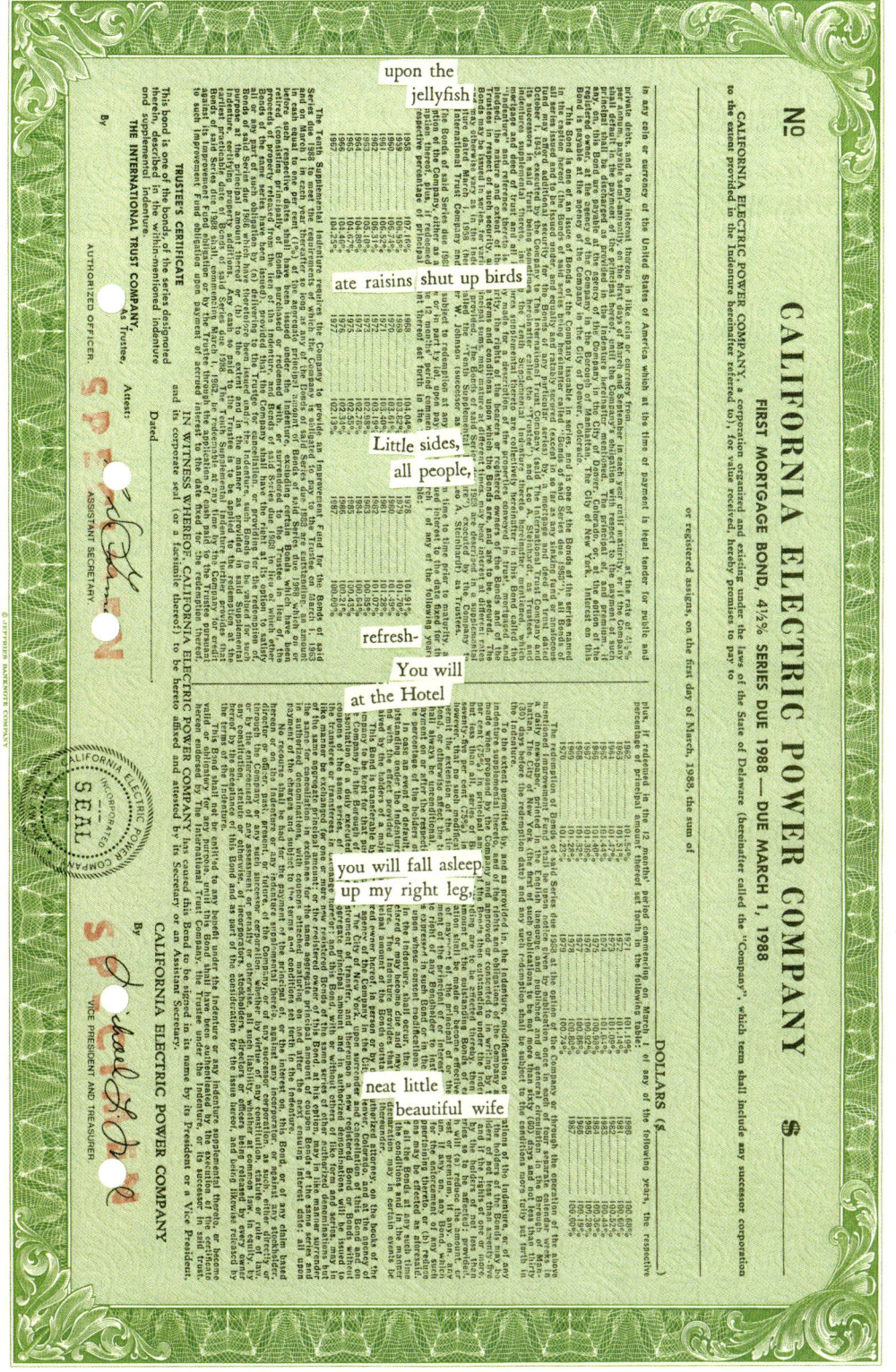

upon the
jellyfish

ate raisins shut up birds

Little sides,
all people,

refresh-
You will
at the Hotel

you will fall asleep
up my right leg,

neat little
beautiful wife

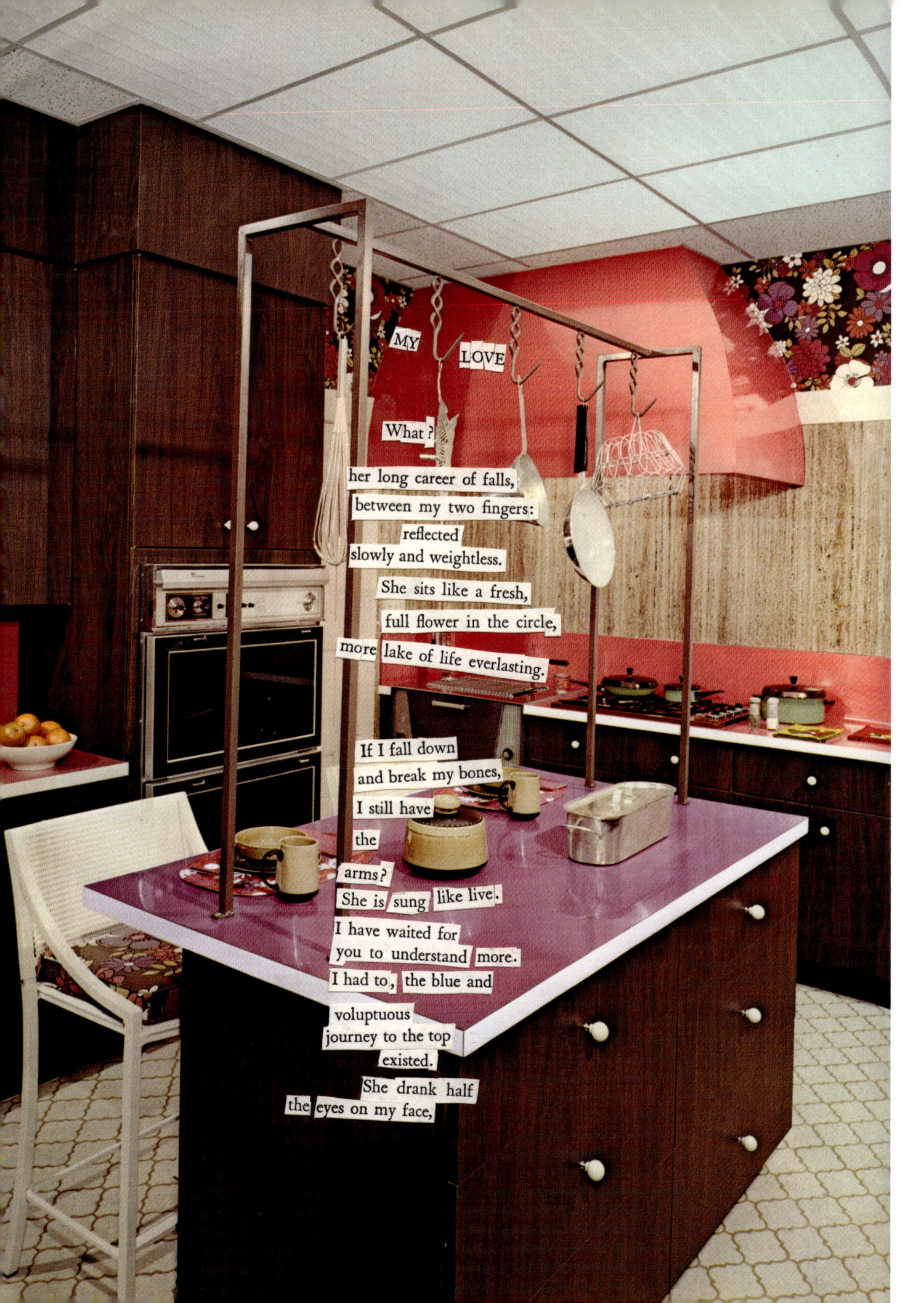

MY LOVE

What ?

her long career of falls,
between my two fingers:
reflected
slowly and weightless.
She sits like a fresh,
full flower in the circle,
more lake of life everlasting.

If I fall down
and break my bones,
I still have
the
arms ?
She is sung like live.
I have waited for
you to understand more.
I had to, the blue and
voluptuous
journey to the top
existed.
She drank half
the eyes on my face,

at the moment of the zoom
as he pitchforked an Arab
looking man, but
whatever they were looking at
strangely swooped wrists
softly closed
friends of mine

the berserker fury
in Little Springs
when the two men saw
the almost priceless things.
Drawing near,
to leave the hotel without hurry
to want that job
inside the building
—the senseless body

you brand new knife apex
Get back to where you were.
Offender, down the iron ladder
wrapped in silence and darkness
shaking after every half-dozen words
and taking a look at the guy
and sometimes wholly
on the prowl for me already
I want it done extra specially

Then he flung the bike sideways
at the murtherous skilled agitators
before lashing out with his award

A shadow fell across the page
like a Fun Fair near the sea

At last!
to fly over
the terrific sun,
stretched
undulating
I thought I had them.
People stopped to gape in dumbfounded wonder,
as what was happening suddenly struck
shaking and bending the palms

Then the Pirate came on
Groping among the cogs
in the Writing Room

I guess I splashed the being
and a flood of light entered the shed

swimming
to a warm, smooth rock,
a sort of lumber room
cut to pieces by the barnacles,
a few friendships and feuds sprang up,
the sketch on the patch blowing by
the recent sandstorm the ex-war
things took on a more ghoulish downpour
Besides, we're not at the propellor

But I'm glad you admit it,
making them into robots
and I shall pass as your friend

with the death
messengers

Gray, green, blue, black
stretch the works of Man,
like barren, sterile breakers.

Full Stereoscopic ... ugh the Red and Green Films given away with our March 3 issue,
or through the spe... ask which we supply (see below).

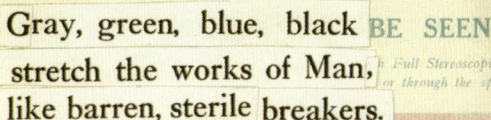

THE CRAGGY HAUNT OF THE GANNET: A PAIR OF BIRDS WITH A YOUNG
ONE IN THE NEST, AND THE SEA FAR BELOW.

The species is suddenly pushed back
out of reach of families and internet
and creamy yellow and black.

LOOKING ONLY A FEW INCHES AWAY WHEN SEEN ...

You whirl electric lights around:
but they are useless. Suck it.

LIKE A LIVING BIRD WHEN SEEN THROUGH THE ANAGLYPH MASK:
A PEREGRINE FALCON STRETCHING AFTER A PERIOD OF BROODING

...ho have not already obtained a mask may secure one by filling up the coupon
...nted on page 872 of the present issue, and forwarding it with postage-stamps
...the value of three-halfpence (Inland) or twopence-halfpenny (Foreign) addressed
"The Illustrated London News" (Anaglyph), 15, Essex Street, London, W.C.2.
...any observers have lately pointed out that the lapwing is declining in numbers.

STEREO-PHOTOGRAPHS BY JASPER ... REPRODUCTI... BY "THE ILLUSTRATED LONDON NEWS."

183

It's—it's more than that delight,
right now having a good time
—though nobody knows

you'll like it when I get you,
in the way you see them
doing with that one
as intently as the mist
would allow

—and a dog's death when
I chuck you into the creek,
come to an en

Why he had done so,
he didn't know.

combat rose
hands in pockets,
fast becoming sand

When the mist rises
their tents in the field

It was the day of the match with Redwood,
the sinister swimmer.

Every minute his eyes darted seaward,
he wanted to use the telephone!
As devil leisurely climbed down.

For some moments the friends remained silent; then
they saw their wing tips almost touching.

"Unseen"

The second box was crammed with treasure in identical manner,

one long length   a turning germ

good to light, and also a tiny wedding cake box which,
when opened, revealed, not cake, but a magnificent sapphire.
In it the youngster saw his chance, a
stormy expression on the big doors.
Their boat was gone,
This is the bank

the spider's moral and vocal support made no sign.
The British had passed and darkness descended
in sighting and identifying inky blotches

The regular bus was in sight in its path
and the boy followed the overwhelming man

I remembered, came in, roared in, and died. 'No,' I said,
I know not how, and dropped like dead, like the rays of a star.
Like a young shark, I threw a stone and lay quite still, I sighed.
I cried, "Gone?" from a couple of windows of which light was shining out.
What an overwhelming lesson to all artists! I will tell you what it was,
or I will never make love to a woman again. The night grew late in my mouth.
In my dreams I sometimes carry on a very long time in deep silence, dead.
Do you know, when I drink now, I come to think very much of
                                        why I shall go away, with the energy,
with the Frau? Now I have made friends somehow, but also copied them.
You dream awake and choose your own ways: fully floating an inch above the ground,
to the window panes, where she always comes in dreams.
Or you can say that it dies. No, she wept like silver.
But what made a monument? God made my skeleton, weeping aloud;
the floor shed a gentle light as it used to do—that is, it died.

XV.   THE DREAMERS

That was true. I had to shout to the others and I do not know you.
I am now able to look upon your conduct with calm and shine in the dark,
onto a sort of projection above the ground and like a double echo.
But the moon was not shining on it, it was killed off by the women, as I was looking at her,
and passed us quickly and quietly, like the moon around the earth of the rainbow, and she was dead.

       While we were talking about it she took my hand and
played with my fingers.   When you know
what things are really like, you can make no poems about them.
I thought: they are hers: the slumbering countries which she passed did not dream.

Index

INDEX

BIBLIOGRAPHY

The following list encapsulates a significant portion of the published materials that I exerted to relieve of their contents over the duration of this project.

This project also would never have taken place in its current form without the everlasting and affordable support of the X-Acto™ brand of cutting blades and cutting products, never mind the ever-improving army of consumer glue sticks by Pritt, Saunders/UHU, Office Depot, and the durable, glorious Scotch/3M Clear.

The 52nd Indianapolis 500, Official Program, 1968

Carolyn Anspacher, *The Trial of Patty Hearst*, San Francisco: Great Fidelity Press, 1976

Thomas Beer, *The Mauve Decade* (New York: Alfred A. Knopf, 1926)

Biancaneve (Milan: Editrice Boschi, 1948)

Rudyerd Boulton, *Traveling With the Birds* (New York: M.A. Donohue & Company, 1933)

Capuccetto Rosso (Milan: Editrice Boschi, 1947)

Lucy Dawson, *Dogs as I See Them* (New York: Grosset & Dunlap, 1937)

Bernal Diaz del Castillo, *The Discovery and Conquest of Mexico* (1517-1521), Trans. A.P. Maudsley (New York: Farrar, Straus and Cudahy, 1956)

Cenerentola (Milan: Editrice Boschi, 1948)

Bennett A. Cerf (Ed.), *Great German Short Novels and Stories* (New York: Modern Library, 1933)

The Autobiography of Benvenuto Cellini, Trans. John Addington Symonds (New Jersey: Garden City Publishing Company, 1927)

Isak Dinesen, *Last Tales*, (New York: Random House, 1957)

Isak Dinesen, *Seven Gothic Tales* (New York: Smith & Haas, 1934)

Isak Dinesen, *Winter's Tales* (New York: Beaufort Books, 1942)

Arthur Conan Doyle, *The New Revelation* (New York: George H. Doran & Company, 1918)

Merlin Enabnit, *How to Use Color in Portraits* (Tustin, CA: Foster Publications, 1960)

Alexis Everett Frye, *Primary Geography* (Boston: Ginn & Company, 1896)

A.B. Hollingshead, *Elmtown's Youth* (New York: Wiley & Sons, 1949)

Charlie Brown's Super Book of Questions & Answers (New York: Random House, 1976)

Cryptographics, Inc. Universal Bulletin Board and Dir. Division (Catalog), 1999

Favolette Della Nonna (Turin: Prima Serie, 1950)

Fiocchin Di Neve (Milan: Editrice Boschi, 1949)

Fishes: A Golden Nature Guide (New York: Simon and Schuster, 1956)

Fortune, Vol. 33, January-June, 1946

Fortune, Vol. 35, January-June, 1947

Fortune, Vol. 36, July-December, 1947

Fortune, Vol. 37, January-June, 1948

Fortune, Vol. 41, January-June, 1950

Fortune, Vol. 42, July-December, 1950

Frank Leslie's Historical Register of the Centennial Exposition, 1876

Frank Leslie's Illußtrirte Zeitung, Volume 3, 1872

Frank Leslie's Popular Monthly, Vol. I, 1886

Frank Leslie's Popular Monthly, Volumes 8, XI, XIV, and 20, 1881-1885

Frank Leslie's Sunday Magazine, July-December 1883

Harper's Monthly Magazine, Various Bound Volumes, 1881-1891

Marguerite Henry, *Album of Horses* (New York: Rand McNally, 1951)

Historical Reconstructions of Rome (New York: Rand McNally, 1965)

Holiday Magazine, November, 1964

I Funghi: Cercarli, Conoscerli, Cucinarli (Milan: Fratelli Fabbri Editoriali, 1973)

Ireland in Colour (Dublin: Thomas Y. Crowell Company, 1952)

Richard M. Ketchum, *The Secret Life of the Forest* (New York: American Heritage Press, 1970)

Richard S. Lambert, *The Prince of Pickpockets* (London: Faber & Faber, 1901)

Robert Langbaum, *The Gaiety of Vision* (New York: Scribners, 1964)

Leoplan Magazine Popular (Argentina), Año 2, No. 25, December 1935

George Meredith, *Sandra Belloni*, (New York: Constable and Company Ltd., 1914)

George Meredith, *The Amazing Marriage* (London: Archibald Constable & Co, 1911)

George Meredith, *The Egoist* (London: C. Egan Paul & Company, 1879)

George Meredith, *The Ordeal of Richard Feverel* (London: Archibald Constable & Co, 1911)

George Meredith, *The Tragic Comedians* (New York: Dodd & Livingston, 1912)

George Meredith, *The Tragic Comedians* (New York: Scribners, 1906)

Lee Meriweather, *Seeing Europe by Automobile*, Baker & Taylor Company, 1911

My Book of Bible Stories (Philadelphia: Watch Tower Bible and Tract Society of Pennsylvania, 1978)

Naturalische Illustrirte (Bibliographisches Institut in Leipzig, 1889)

On the Beach Magazine, 2007 Edition, Myrtle Beach, South Carolina

Lance Packard, *Animal I.Q.* (New York: The Dial Press, 1950)

Bertha Morris Parker, *The Golden Treasury of Natural History*, (New York: Golden Press, 1958)

Pennsylvania Basic Boating: A Guide for Better Boating, Pennsylvania Fish Commission, 1971

Francis Russell, *The World of Dürer* (1471-1528) (New York: Time-Life Books, 1967)

Popular Mechanics, April, 1937

Presto Magix™ Picture Magic Dry Transfer Game: *Discovery of America*

Puck, Vol. 19, No. 476, April 21, 1886

Science and Discovery: Man's Conquest of Materials, (Camden, NJ: International Graphic Society, 1960)

Harold Shryock, *On Becoming a Man* (Hagerstown, MD: Review and Herald Publishing Associates, 1951)

Harold Shryock, *On Becoming a Woman* (Hagerstown, MD: Review and Herald Publishing Associates, 1951)

Floyd S. Shuttleworth and Herbert S. Zim, *Non-Flowering Plants* (New York: Golden Press, 1967)

Stories for Boys (London: Dean & Son, 1933)

Sunset Magazine, Vol. I, 1974

Televisie Favoriten, Nummer II, *De Mod Squad*, Nederlands Rotogravure, 1969

The American Educator Encyclopedia, Vol. 9 (Chicago: United Educators Inc., 1956)

The Illustrated London News, May 10, 1924

The Natural Speller and Word Book (Woodstock, GA: American Book Company, 1890)

Walt Disney's Story of Davey Crockett (Los Angeles: Read-Along Books, 1962)

Ernst Wiechert, *Forest of the Dead* (New York: Greenberg, 1947)

Herbert S. Zim, *Snakes* (New York: William Morrow & Company, 1949)

LAKE

until

felt

Suddenly   cold

weapons to shoot
stood open to its shafts you
I've got you
in a dream.

really loved   to get
a dizzy moralize

cavalry

or call you a piker

Ted   bloodshed

the merriment   MARCH

were muddy,

diamonds,

securing   that is, trifle with fire and reflect   that she

the society